The Lock-House 1

By

Rachel Hayward

Author: Rachel Hayward
Email: thelockhousehaunting@outlook.com

Chantry List:

4 Harold Simmonds (1959) Emily Burroughs (1956) Blanche Emma Holt (1963)
   Doris Butterworth (1985) Edith Thornton (1997)
5 Agnes Akyere Wallace (2001)   Kathleen Moore (2010)
6 John Harold Giles *Priest* (1920)   Alice Elizabeth Spargo (1981)
7 Maria D'Arcy Guy Jerdein (1940) Sydney Pollard (1936)
   Mary Charman (1956)
8 Constance Ritchie 1939)   Vera Jackson (1992)
9 William Jones (1924)   Philip Barrington Simeon *Priest* (1926)
   Maud Broughton (1985)
10 Reginald Cole (1940)   Evelyn White (1968) Eric Jones (1992)

Please inform Fr. Amos or the Churchwardens immediately
if anyone is taken into hospital or advise them if anyone is taken ill.

Vicar:
The Revd Fr. Colin J. Amos SSC
S. Augustine's Vicarage
Kilburn Park Road
London, NW6 5XB   020 7624 1637   fr.amos@sky.com

Honorary Assistant Priest:
Fr. David Cherry   07939 553547   davidcherry2015@gmail.com

Assistant Curate ~ Self Supporting Ministry
Fr. Stephen Brown

Church Wardens:
Mandisa Baleka :   07904 961014
Glyn Williams   :   020 7286 6893   glyn.williams1@btinternet.com

Please take this Newsletter home with you.
Do take a spare copy to anybody who cannot be here today
or for a neighbour or friend.

Keep up to date with the Parish's News & Calendar
www.saugustinekilburn.org.uk

Take a look at the See of Fulham Website
www.bishopoffulham.org.uk

The Society

The Votive Lamps for this Week

The Seven Sanctuary Lamps
are sponsored by Mandisa Baleka
and burn to the Glory of God
and in Loving Memory of her cousin Nomonde Mestile
on her first Year's Mind.

The S. Michael Sanctuary Lamp
is sponsored by Pauline Cyrus
and burns to the Glory of God
and for the healing of Peter Wakefield & Olive Blake.

The Our Lady of Walsingham Votive Lamp
is sponsored by Joseph & Matilda Mathias
and burns to the Glory of God
and for Charles

To sponsor the lamps please see Fr. Amos - the 7 Sanctuary lamps 7 days
(minimum donation £25) or one of the 7 day Votive Lamps(minimum donation £5)

We are on Twitter ! Follow us at:

@StAugustineNW6

Dates for your diary:

TOMORROW - Monday 5th December 7.30 pm Fr. Brown's first mass
followed by refreshments in High School.
Thursday 8th December 5.30 pm Primary School Full Governing Body.
Tuesday 13th December 7.00pm High School Carol Service – All welcome
Friday 16th December 9.30am Primary School Carol Service – All welcome

Christmas Eve:
5.00pm Crib Service – suitable for all children – and adults
11.30 pm Midnight Mass in candlelight.

Christmas Day:
10.30 am – Solemn High Mass.

Calendar

5th	Monday	7.30 pm	Fr. Brown's first mass.
6th	Tuesday	~ S. Nicholas	
		8.00 am	Mass
7th	Wednesday ~ S. Ambrose		
		12.00 noon	Mass
8th	Thursday	~ The Immaculate Conception of BVM	
		8.00am	Mass
9th	Friday	6.00 pm	Mass
10th	Saturday	12.00 noon	Mass

11th Sunday ~ Advent III

        8.00am Mass

        10.30am   Solemn Mass

        6.00 pm   Evensong

Welcome to Bishop Jonathan as he celebrates mass and ordains Deacon Brown to the priesthood and Licenses Fr. Cherry to the parish.
Welcome also to the Archdeacon Fr. Luke, to Fr. Neil Evans as Post Ordination Training Officer and the Rev'd Prebendary Andrew Davies as preacher along with all visitors and guests for these celebrations. We look forward to continuing the welcome over refreshments served afterwards at the back of the church. Thank you to all who have assisted in the same.

Fr. Brown's First Mass will be offered tomorrow at 7.30pm followed by refreshments in the High School All are welcome and encouraged to attend.

Advent Pop Up Stalls continue today please support these as all proceeds go to the Heating Project. By their nature, if you wish to 'pop up' a stall next week then please do, and so on through Advent.
Donations to the Christmas Hamper are welcomed – tickets now available for this so please take some to sell / purchase yourself – thank you.

Heating Project Gifts still needed to cover the final £690.00
The power and effect of the heating is being felt – but – *please, we need to pay for it* ! So, all donations and fundraising remain dedicated to that aim. Please give your donations to Fr. Amos, the Churchwardens or Treasurer ASAP so we can completely enjoy – project finished – by Christmas ?!
Organ Humidifier whilst unseen some £2,000.00 of work was undertaken on urgent repairs to this last month. If anybody would like to contribute towards this protection and maintenance of the organ please see Fr. Amos or Wardens.

Welcome to
S. Augustine's Kilburn

Sunday 4th December 2016 AD

Advent II

10.30am Solemn Mass with
Ordination & Licensing
6.00pm Evensong

Hymns at Mass: Please see Order of Service.

Do stay for a drink and chat after Mass

If you are visiting for the first time please do fill in a 'welcome card'
(available from the sidespersons or on the stand as you enter the Church) and
give it to the Church wardens or priest at the end of mass.

Special Blessings are welcome Requests for these are to be made on a simple
form available on the stand as you enter Church and are to be given to the
Church Wardens prior to the start of the 10.30 am Mass.

Sunday School is available for over 5 year olds in the Parish Room.
Under 5's are welcome with a parent or guardian remaining present to
supervise them. Please bring your children to the Parish Room for 10.25 am.

Communion is brought to the front row of the Nave for anyone who does not
wish or feels unable to climb the Chancel steps. You are welcome to come to
the Altar Rail via the Ambulatory if that safely assists you.

Kindly note:
No wandering around is permitted during Mass.
Should toilet facilities be required please see the Wardens.
All mobile phones should be switched to 'silent'. *Thank you.*

Dedication

This book is dedicated to all those I have known and have helped to enrich my life, both living and passed. To my mother, whose diaries proved to be invaluable; to Andrew, Coral and Abigail whose patience was remarkable while I have hidden away to write this. To my father, who has proved such a wonderful and profound influence on my life. I would also like to thank Shirley for her account of the apparition and Ian Pethers for his photograph showing the old weir before it was rebuilt. Then finally, to the Dean Writers Circle which, without their encouragement and inspiration meant I would never have put pen to paper in the first place.

"I think a person who is thus terrified with the Imagination of Ghosts and Spectres much more reasonable, than one who is contrary to the reports of all Historians sacred and profane, ancient and modern, and to the traditions of all nations, thinks the appearance of Spirits fabulous and groundless."

- Joseph Addison, the Spectator 1711

Forward

Many people have asked me why I have written this book and it is, in itself a very good question. I am not rich or famous and the vast majority of this world has never heard of me. Yet I am positive that the experiences that I am about to share with you are not unique to me. I am not the only person that has lived on an island, I am not the only person that has lived by a river and I am sure that I am not the only person who has had a special relationship with their surroundings and its inhabitants. The fact that some of the inhabitants that I shared my home with were not living and not all welcome does make this book slightly different but again, I know I am not the only person to have seen and lived with ghosts and spirits.

In no way is this book an attempt to change anyone's beliefs, religion or ideas and other than my mother's diaries much of it I have no way of proving. But, I promise you that every word that I have written is true and all I ask is that you keep an open mind.

So in answer to the question that so many have asked my answer is this: Whilst I was growing up most people refused to believe what I had witnessed and so I stopped telling people. Not being able to share my experiences made me very lonely and if just one person reads this book and is left feeling that at last there is someone out there who would believe them, then I have succeeded.

Now please, read on and enjoy.

A bird's eye view of Cookham Lock, taken in the early 1980's.
(Copyright © Fay Andrews)

Chapter 1- The Beginning

(Firstly, a thought for the reader:
It is a theory that is seriously deliberated by Paranormal Experts and investigators alike that water could be capable of holding and remembering people's thoughts and emotions. It is also a fact that water covers 70% of our planet. So it is worth considering and could go a long way to explain why apparitions and paranormal phenomena have been documented all over our World. The following account also lends itself to this theory although it is not a theory I knew anything about whilst growing up. Dear Reader, it is for you to draw whatever conclusion you choose.)

Such was the magic and the revolutionary history that enveloped the period that I was born that I live in the hope of being classed as a sixties child! My adventure started at the end of that decade when after being surprised several months earlier by the fact that she was pregnant my mother gave birth to me on the 14th of November 1969. So, although I was never able to wear the miniskirts of Mary Quant, in my mind a sixties child I am and shall always be.

It is only, as it always is, with hindsight that I now truly appreciate how unbelievably lucky I was. The first twenty or so years of my life were quite unique and if it were not for the place that I grew up in along with the very special family and friends that surrounded me I would not be the person I am today.

I was born into the niche world of lock keeping on the River Thames and in those days although they were hard days they were also good days. Damn good in fact. My parents discovered the magic of the river whilst on their honeymoon many years before. They had hired a boat and were enjoying the scenic tranquility of the River Thames. Little did they know then that the lock that they found so beautiful and idyllic hidden in the depths of Berkshire would one day become their home?

My father began his career on the river further downstream at Old Windsor Lock and this was to become my parent's home for several years. It was here that my two brothers discovered the life of fishing and boating and when Cookham Lock became available my parents grabbed the opportunity and applied for the posting. Needless to say the lock was awarded to my father and in the year of 1967 they moved in and as you now know, two years later I arrived. My brothers by this time were twelve and fourteen years my senior and from what I have heard, they were not overly delighted at my arrival! I understand however, that my oldest brother Neil was slightly more pleased with the idea of having a baby sister than my other brother David was.

For those who have never travelled through Cookham Lock nor have passed through it since the late eighties our lives could have been seen as almost alien. The lock itself sits between two islands. Originally there was just one island but when the lock was built in 1766 because the river there was considered too dangerous, a channel was cut through and the lock was built between.

The islands were my life. They were my garden, my Eden. Sashes Island is the larger of the two and also holds the trophy for being the largest island on the Thames. Its' smaller sister Formosa, was where our house was actually located. The islands covered an approximate total area of over eighty acres and were a mixture of open grazing land, scrubland and dense thicketed areas. Throughout both islands there were a huge diversity of trees and flowers. The trees ranged from graceful willows, holly and elder to the majestic oak, horse chestnut and beech. In those very early days we also had a good collection of elm trees; that was of course until in 1970 when the Dutch elm disease swept across the county almost wiping out the species to extinction. I particularly remember three of these trees that stood almost as watchmen over the upper part of the main island and as a toddler being able to find the most fantastically sized and deliciously tasting field mushrooms beneath the cool shade of their boughs. I believe that they were some of the last to be destroyed and I remember crying when their majestic forms came crashing down.

These islands were strictly private and there was no admittance except with permission. Other than our home, a large barn used for storing hay and straw and the lock office there were no other buildings on the islands. Ours was the only house and our nearest neighbours were on the mainland; a good twenty minutes' walk away. Vehicular access to the mainland was by way of the weir and to cross the weir you had to pass through a pair of locked gates. The gates were surrounded by barbed wire and as very few dared pass round them for fear of either being heavily scratched by the wire or falling to the waters below, our island was safe.

A local farmer used to rent the land for his cattle and sheep and in those early days I looked after his two horses. By the age of five I could often be seen (if there was anyone there to see me) riding Winston, a massive Stallion, bareback through the fields.

I had more dens than anyone could imagine, I knew where to catch the biggest fish and I knew where each type of bird and animal made its home. I could show you foxes dens, badgers sets, where the kingfishers hunted, where the kestrels nested, where the trout sunbathed, where you could watch a 40lb pike feed. I could go on but this book is not just about the wildlife.

As you may have noticed I use the word 'I' a lot. This was because it really was just me or at first so I thought. My brothers were not into playing with their young sister that much and I had no friends. It sounds sad but it was true. I started nursery school late in life. This was not the fault of my parents but the local council. It was one of many problems of living on an island. You see, one side of the mainland was Berkshire and the other was Buckinghamshire. In those days there were no postcodes and we didn't pay council tax because we didn't have any amenities. When it came to my education Buckinghamshire Council said we came under Berkshire and Berkshire responded equally. When I was very young my mother used to work at the local corner shop in the nearby village and whilst chatting to a customer she revealed this dilemma to the lady she was serving. It turned out that the customer was indeed a Lady - no less than Lord Young's wife and it was her intervention whilst sitting at the House of Lords that resolved this situation.

When I did eventually start school matters did not improve for some time. Although I did have friends at school none ever came back to my house for tea or to play. Their parents were too scared that their children would fall into the river and drown! Although I remember it saddening me it did not bother me too much. Once I started primary school, friends became more inquisitive about how I lived and it was not long before their nagged parents relented and I could show others my magical world.

My father may have also played a part in helping the situation by providing the school with various types of boats for us to play in. He came by these as he said "By salvage rights!" Often, especially during the winter months when the river was in full flood and had broken its banks, boats would become trapped on our weirs after breaking free of their moorings. Dad would rescue them and leave them in front of our garden waiting for the owners to claim them. If no one came forward then we would use them for our own purposes, sell them, or if they were suitable donate them to a good cause, namely my primary school!

Although all loved the islands my home was a different matter entirely. In 1836 the lock house was built and it stayed in its original condition until my father retired in 1993. By then it was a grade 2 listed building but in such need of repair that a large portion of it had to be taken down brick by brick, made habitable for the next lockkeeper and then rebuilt using the same bricks.

It is now a warm, modern and comfortable abode but when we lived there, well let's just say it was home. Our home consisted of a large kitchen with the bathroom just off to the right and another room at the end of the kitchen that was the airing cupboard. This, in actual fact was mainly used to house an enormous amount of dog food for our dogs that we kept and as a birthing room for them when they had puppies. (More of them later.) The remainder of the downstairs consisted of a fairly sized lounge and dining room with two other smaller rooms and a large cupboard under the stairs. Upstairs there was a tiny bedroom immediately to the right (this was my first room) with my Brother David's room leading directly off it. In front of the stairs was my parent's room and at the end of the landing to the left was my oldest brother Neil's room.

There was no heating upstairs so in the summer it was always cool but in the winter it was freezing and I do mean freezing. Neil's bedroom faced the river and in the depths of winter it could become unbearable. It was not unknown for hot water bottles to freeze solid in the bed and icicles to hang from the light bulb! Downstairs the heat came from the Rayburn in the kitchen and an open log fire in the lounge.

As far as luxuries were concerned we did have them but by God you missed them when they didn't work. There were no main gas pipes to the island so our gas came in the form of gas bottles. There were no sewage pipes to take our waste away just one pipe that led to a cesspit not far from the house. This was emptied every six months by a vessel belonging to the Thames Conservancy which I believe was lovingly called 'Lavender Lill.' We had no postal service; we had to walk a mile and a half to the local garage to collect our post. We had no street lights so torches were a must. We also had no rubbish collection. Our rubbish was disposed of by digging a big pit towards the edge of the island and land filling our refuge. When the hole was filled up or the rats became too big we set fire to it. When the hole was completely filled it was covered over and another one was dug. In today's world of reduce, reuse, recycle this seems to me now a horrendous way to carry on but back then it was the norm.

We also did not have any mains water. What we did have however, was an underground stream that ran directly beneath the house and water was pumped up electrically. This was fine until there was a power cut but even now I would still rather drink that water than any I have ever tasted since.

It was not just the living conditions that made life at the lock so unusual it was the way of life itself. A way of life that I found completely normal until, of course, the friends that I made invited me back to their homes. Then I discovered what an odd life we led.

Firstly there were our dogs. My mother used to breed Pyrenean Mountain dogs and including the puppies it was not uncommon for there to be up to twenty five of them meandering round the lock-side at any given period. Only one was ever kept tied up although in honesty I wondered why we ever bothered. Dusty was kept tethered in the garden. His tether was actually a thirty foot rope attached to a huge length of anchor chain which was dug into the ground. I am sure that in a previous life he used to be Houdini because even this did not stop him from escaping. Now you may wonder where was there for him to go because after all we lived on an island? This fact however never stopped him and it became an almost regular occurrence for my dad to receive a phone call from any of the local police stations to say that the dog had been brought in complete with rope and chain. How he ever managed to swim across the river with that additional weight I will never know. In the end, because my parents were so worried that he would drown they re-homed with a lovely family who had a large amount of land that was surrounded by a huge wall. He was content to live the rest of his days there and never tried to escape again.

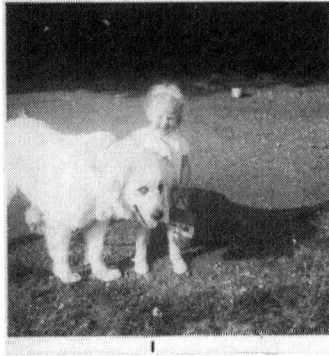

Me & 'Elsa.' This picture was taken in the summer of 1972

Then of course there was the river herself. From Easter to September the river and the islands were a hive of activity. In those days boaters flocked to the river, it was a hugely popular holiday destination and my father would often be working from dawn to dust and beyond. The queues of boats at either end of the lock would never seem to have an end and as many owned their own boats we would see the same people throughout the summer. The River became our street. It gave us companionship and entertainment. It was like one long party with the occasional gatecrasher.

But then, when autumn reared its head and the high winds and torrential rains came causing the river to break its banks and the water to roar through the weirs as if possessed by the very devil itself, our lives turned to that of almost complete solitude. Boats would be forbidden from leaving their moorings and no boats meant no people. If it wasn't for the fact that we had to leave the island to go shopping, go to work and go to school we would never see a soul for six months.

My brothers could entertain themselves. My early memories of the two giants were generally happy ones. Neil had a penchant for fast cars and these took up a lot of his time and in the end would prove to be his downfall. He was an outgoing young man with a wide group of friends. David was somewhat shyer but although they were both very different in many ways they were exactly the same. David's love of vehicles came in the two wheeled variety but where Neil was outgoing David was never happier unless he was out fishing or hunting with his twelve bore and his ferrets by his feet.

If I am honest I would say that they tolerated me but only just. Neil, although further in age was closer to me and I have vague recollections of us ganging up against David. Locking him in his bedroom thus forcing him to escape through his window, I seem to remember was a favourite.

By the year of 1976 both of them were working; Neil at a local boatyard and David for the local council. But for me when it was too cold and wet to go outside I opted for books. I was then and am still an avid reader although in those days I had so much more time.

It was in the October of that year when it all changed and really where this book begins. In the first week of that month our last Pyrenean died and then one week later on a particularly dark evening I had come home from school to an almost empty house. It was not unusual because as far as I was concerned both my brothers were at work and it was just I and my parents in the house. My mum loved this time of day it was the only time when she had any peace from her children.

It was getting dark when I noticed a car's headlights coming down our lane. The car came slowly as the road was so full of potholes it took a lot of navigation. I thought it must be Neil returning home from work as David rode a motor bike. But it wasn't. It was our local police.

My eldest brother had not come home the night before but we didn't think anything of this and had just presumed he gone on to work from wherever he had spent the night. Tragically this was not the case and our local police had the awful duty of informing a family who were not only well thought of members of the community but also friends that their son had been killed in a car crash.

The death of my brother hit me the same way I suppose that it would hit most nearly seven year old girls. I accepted it with innocent bluntness and apparently when I was told I was more insistent on telling my parents what I had had for lunch at school that day. I remember my brother's funeral though, primarily because I wasn't allowed to go. I spent the day I think at school and then went home to my cousin's house. That experience was slightly unnerving because they lived in a house that possessed a turret and that is where I spent the night. Now most little girls would love the idea of spending the night in a castle tower but it was not an experience that I enjoyed. My cousin spent the evening telling me horrid stories and as the room in the tower was dark and eerie I did not get much sleep that night.

Returning home back to a forced normality gave me my first insight into spiritual thinking. One afternoon I asked my mother if we could go and visit my brother but she said no. She explained to me all about dying and the soul going to heaven. 'Did everyone go to heaven,' I had asked and was most surprised to learn that as long as you had been good in life then yes, everyone went to heaven. 'What about our dog, did she go to heaven as well'? Patiently my mum explained that she believed and so did a lot of other people that all animals went to heaven. 'So,' I concluded everyone who is good and dies and every animal that dies go to heaven?' 'Yes,' she confirmed and then wearily encouraged me to go off and play.

Looking back now I can see what difficult questions they were to a mummy who had just lost her eldest son but my brain had so many more questions to ask and childish intuition told me not to pester any more. And so I thought. Everyone is a lot, an awful lot. Everyone is the total of everyone who has ever lived, right back to when apes first stood up on two legs. In fact everyone then becomes everything, all the dogs, cats, horses, cows, apes, tigers and then all the fish, birds, spiders, ants wasps, and then what about the dinosaurs? It was all too much for me and didn't make sense simply because heaven just could not be that big. Even if it is not the actual bodies of these animals but just their souls there would simply just not be enough room. And obviously religion didn't come into it. My dog was never religious. My cat certainly never put her paws together to meow grace before tucking into a freshly caught squirrel. No, I had concluded this would take a lot more thinking about. The answers came to me at our school library.

I loved libraries especially our school one but it was the only part of school that I enjoyed. My first school was a convent and there I was bullied relentlessly. I was forever coming home with bruises from where I had been kicked or hit but the library like the chapel was conducted in total silence. Here I could escape the taunts (the latest was that my brother had died to get away from me) and spend the lunchtimes hiding in books. I always sat directly in front of Sister Agnes so that if anyone did come in to find me she would protect me from them.

It was here that I read about the Native Americans and their seven stages of life and how reincarnation played such an important role in their beliefs. I could not get to read too much of it because Sister Agnes saw me reading it and said it went against the teachings of the Roman Catholics and it was therefore not suitable. (I often wondered why if it was not suitable, was it in the library?) It did not stop me reading it at our local library though a year or so later. So for the time being I had to content myself with my own thoughts and deliberations.

Now, as would be expected the death of my eldest brother crushed my family for some time leaving my father to hold us all together. David threw himself into his work and his motorbikes and would then spend all of his spare time out in the fields hunting with his ferrets. Dad spent as much time on the lock as possible and also took up coach driving to earn some extra money and my mother opened a small but strangely deceptive in size, sell anything shop for the happy boaters. While there were boats about the shop was open and its closing time was often not until my parents went to bed which was usually way past midnight.

When I read through my mother's diary of 1977 one thing is very apparent, everyone was grieving and all separately. Hindsight makes me wonder how our family survived and if I am honest about it I wonder if our survival did not have rather a lot to do with me. As the youngest in the house it seems that my parents spare time was always spent taking me swimming, taking me to my friends' homes and then collecting me from wherever I happened to be. Although I always seemed to be going somewhere I always seemed to be missed when I wasn't at home.

Although the precise date is not clear to me it was sometime in the early part of 1977 that we welcomed a new addition to our not so happy family. Neil was a hugely popular lad and was greatly missed by his many friends. Speaking to some of them much later in life they had felt their lives ripped apart and in those days there was no counselling for bereaved mates. As young men they were just expected 'to get on with it.'   I think it must have been that sense of loss and the need to show how they felt that led them to do a very wonderful thing. They all clubbed together and gave my parents some money. Now when I say some money I mean a sum of approximately £600.00. A huge amount in those days and their suggestion for its use was eagerly accepted. With this money my mum and daddy went out and bought a puppy. However, it was not just any puppy but a St Bernard puppy. Neil was six feet seven inches tall and this had earned him the nickname of Tiny. It seemed only fitting that this gorgeous bundle of fur be named the same.

It was also decided to upgrade my sleeping arrangements. Neil's room was decorated and all my bits and bobs moved in. I now had a bedroom that you could, as long as it was not a very big one, swing a cat in!

It is also my belief that another reason for me spending so much time away from home that year was to do with that old phrase of peace and quiet. After Neil's death the relationship between David and me disintegrated. We could not be in the same room together for more than a couple of minutes before an argument would ensue. There was no other way to describe him except to say that in those days he was a bully and we hated each other with all the passion we could muster. The problem was that he being twelve years older than me and being decidedly larger than me meant that I stood no chance in any of the many fights with him. It was guaranteed that when he and I were in the same room all hell would break loose and I would be the one in tears.

Most people remember the year of 1977 as the year that saw the film Star Wars blast onto the silver screen and the year we celebrated our Queens Silver Jubilee. Although I remember the Silver Jubilee very well, indeed we were honoured for Her Majesty travelled though our lock on a particularly wet day and spent time chatting to my father and acknowledging me with a personal wave and smile. However, I was dealing with other things. Not long after I had moved into my new bedroom I found out that I was sharing it with an uninvited guest. The problem I had was that nobody believed me.

As I have said previously, my room was not that large. Walking in through the door which was situated on the right side of the room, directly in front as you entered sat my large dressing table. It was traditionally shaped with drawers at both end and a large, round mirror in the centre. One end was pushed up against the far wall which held the window that looked out over the lock. To the left of the door was my wardrobe and opposite the dressing table was my bed. Other than the bin originally that was all that the room contained so my parents couldn't understand when I said that this visitor stood in the corner of the room by the dressing table. The truth was that he stood in the corner of the room *in* the dressing table.

I remember him as clearly as if it were yesterday when he first appeared. His black hair so short it looked like it had been cut with a small dish on his head and his deep, dark eyes that twinkled in the fading light of the day. He was older than me maybe eleven or twelve and he was very, very slim. On every occasion that I saw him his dress was always identical. Dark coloured trousers and a jacket that did up to the neck with a short collar that stood up instead of lying flat. The fact that he was standing there was bad enough; I knew he shouldn't be there and every time I went to bring my parents up to see him he would give me a cheeky wave and upon my return the only thing I could show my parents, fresh air!

I am positive that he was in my room long before I saw him. Every night after I had gone to bed I could hear whispering. It was never loud enough to make out words; all I could hear was a constant human mumble. I use to lie in bed with my face to the wall terrified of what I would see if I turned over and when I eventually gained the courage and looked, there was nothing and nobody. But I could still hear it. I knew, absolutely knew the sound was from my room and not from either outside or anywhere else in the house. The walls were too thick and even if I yelled at the top of my voice no-one would come as they never heard me.

Then after a while I saw him but to start with he never uttered a word. He just stared and each time I saw him his 'visit' lasted a little longer. After a few weeks of just watching me he spoke. At first he was pleasant enough and we spoke of my school and my friends. I am not sure who brought the subject of my brother up but we did end up discussing him and would agree with me about my grievances with him. After a week or so he became more menacing and began telling me that I should get my own back on him and then people would have to believe me about how horrible my brother really was. He started suggesting that I should do things, things to make people take notice. Most of what he said I disagreed with because even then I knew that hurting people was wrong and my mum and dad had been hurt enough but one night his constant goading got the better of me and I relented.

I used to own a beautiful bronze coloured alarm clock, the traditional sort with two bells at the top and a hammer that, at the appointed time would move quickly from side to side striking the bells deafeningly as it did so. This night he suggested that I throw it through the bedroom window. I did as I was told but I misunderstood him and this infuriated him immensely. He meant for me to hurl it literally through the windows so that the glass would smash but I threw it so that it went through fresh air. It ended up in a mangled heap by the lock and my father was none too pleased, so much so that I was smacked hard for this apparent, unreasonable vandalism.

It was after this episode that my mum dragged me to see our local doctor who could find nothing wrong with me and suggested I was attention seeking. To this day I do not know if my doctor's diagnosis was correct but I know what I saw and when after a couple of days later I screamed at this boy to go away because he wasn't really my friend he stuck his tongue out at me and instantly vanished before my eyes. I never saw him again and the funny thing was that in the weeks that he was in my room although he knew my name he never told me his.

I am not sure if this next incident is related in any way to the boy but as it occurred only a couple of days after he had pulled a face at me and left I do wonder if there was a connection. I am more prone to surmise that the boy was not a boy at all but a manifestation of something more malevolent that appeared in a form that I would find more appealing?

Quite simply I was sound asleep one night in bed when I was violently awoken. I woke up terrified to find myself lying across my dressing table. I think I had been almost ceremoniously dumped on it because it was the very sensation of landing on it that woke me. Confused and frightened I rolled off of it and crawled back into bed but I was hurting. I turned on my bedside light and got out of bed. Lifting my nightdress and peering into my mirror I could see two red marks on the back of my shoulders and then looking down I saw identical marks beginning to appear behind my knees. They corresponded exactly to the edges of the dressing table and by the following day they had changed from welts into bruises. I tried to tell my parents about them but my father's retort was "Don't be so bloody ridiculous!"   I began then to feel very much alone and even at such a young age knew that help from a grown up would not be forth coming.

Chapter 2 - 1978

This was a year that I struggle to remember and even with the help of photographs most of my memories from this year are vague and so I expect this chapter to be quite short. There were three memorable occasions, two of which could be loosely classed as being related to this book but some may say otherwise and so I will not try and force the issue. The third occurrence I had forgotten about until I read my mother's diary and then the events surrounding that time came flooding back but other than these happenings that is all I basically remember. I do not remember my birthday or Christmas. I do not especially remember any of the holidays. The only other 'major' milestone that this year offered was my introduction to adult television. By adult television I mean the transition from children's programmes to the more grown-up type primarily, 'Blake's 7.' I became completely transfixed with its renegade, Anti-Federation heroes, and it was the one night of the week where I was allowed to stay up past my bedtime and watch it. I think it also helped that my father enjoyed the programme as well and it became a regular viewing slot in our home until its heart-breaking demise a few years later.

We started the year by going on holiday to Tenerife, one of the Canary Islands. Whether it was coincidence or planned I do not recall but we were travelling on the same plane with my, at the time best friend and her parents. We were not in the same hotel but they were in close proximity and so I had a fun holiday and spent a lot of time with my friend mainly in the hotel pool where I taught myself to swim.

Back in good old England the warm weather was slow to arrive and we were plagued by cold spells that should have long since left the spring months. If it wasn't cold and cloudy it was raining heavily and it was on once such occasion that my first encounter with lightning took place. I often wonder now if the near misses I had with this type of dangerous weather condition were more than just coincidences and whether or not some higher being was maybe trying to tell me something?

At the point where the road from the weir came onto our island the land could have been seen as being divided into two. Below the weir the island was (except for around its perimeter and where the lock was situated) cleared of trees and was mainly grass and of course, our home but above the weir the area was only maintained by the many grazing animals that the farmer had in situ and was referred to by my family as the Paddock. Therefore trees, shrubs and bushes were predominant. Willow, Beech, Silver Birch and Horse Chestnut trees lined the banks and seemed to keep the Blackberry, Dog Rose and Elder shrubs in check and under constant surveillance. It was here, amongst the wilds of the paddock that I had my playground. It was in the centre area that I had my largest den. I had many other dens around the paddock area and all other than this one was were situated near the edge. In those I could find solitude and either fish or just watch the river and its inhabitants without interruption from family or disrupting the animals that I was regarding.

My main den was easy to find, mainly because of its size. It consisted of a large circular group of Elder bushes and Creeping Willow trees that gave cool protection if the weather became too warm and a certain amount of dryness for the wetter days. The dry areas were not because the leaves kept the rain out but more to do with the fact that I had acquired several plastic bin liners for some of the floor area and also a couple of old tarpaulins which I had fixed to the trees with bailing twine. Within the den I had a small storage area for food and drinks, a couple of upturned bottle crates with a plank of wood on that made a very good bench and a small cooking area, yes a fire (if my dad had known he would have killed me) for toasting bread and heating up cans of baked beans and water for cups of tea. With both my parents so busy it was never hard to 'borrow' the odd items from our larder!

Although I stated that this den was easy to find it was not easy to enter. Not only did (if a friend came to play)one require a password which, just to be on the safe side would change daily but also the entrance was well hidden and in the summer when the leaves were out in full it was virtually impossible to find. I had fashioned a 'gate' which incorporated some of the more bendy branches of the trees and surrounding foliage and only I knew how to open it without getting scratched to pieces by the brambles or whipped by some of the longer, slender twigs. Pushing the 'gate' open from the inside was fairly easy but to gain access from outside the gate meant using two carefully camouflaged lengths of string. It was I have to admit even now, a clever invention.

One afternoon I had left this den to go fishing at the far point of the island and it had started to rain. Actually it was raining very heavily, the clouds had become the colour of slate and the river was choppy with the wind that was gusting down the lock cut and weir stream. It was then that I noted something rather odd. On the other side of the river it wasn't raining. Where I stood under the shelter of a Horse Chestnut by the river bank I could clearly see the Ferry Inn opposite and it was quite evident that there it was bone dry. This, for some reason unnerved me and so I decided to pack up my tackle and go home.

I had nearly reached the road that went to the weir when thunder erupted above me. I had not heard it rumble across the sky, it was as if it had built up directly where it crashed and seconds later forked lightening split through the clouds and the rain became torrential. I ran for cover under another Horse Chestnut but as this tree was already drenched it gave very little shelter and I decided to just go home as quickly as possible. It was only a matter of seconds since I had left the tree when the lightening came again and this time it seemed to have a destination in mind. With either exacting accuracy or pure chance it struck the tree I had been sheltering under only moments before. I stood transfixed and watched as this mighty giant who had supplied me with a countless source of the very best quality conkers could do nothing except give in to the power of the electricity and come thundering down onto the now sodden ground below. Although I felt a great sadness in its passing its use did not cease there. My father spent many hours after work with his chain saw and it became a wonderful source of warmth the following winter.

A similar incident occurred towards the end of the year but to my knowledge this tree still remains standing. One early, dark evening for some strange reason I wanted to join my brother night fishing.

He did not want me to go with him as he said that I would frighten the fish away but my dad said I could run after him and join him. Once I was there my brother probably wouldn't mind.

The weather was foul and as I left the house the rain, thunder and lightening were already in full Tempest mode. Back then I didn't wear glasses but my vision was impeded by the wind as it used my hair to whip my face. With that and the rain that was coming down with the fierceness of tiger's claws I was amazed that I managed to cross the lock gates without incident. I reached the bottom of the lock and stood under an Oak Tree trying to work out which way my brother had gone. At the very moment I decided that night fishing in that weather was not a good plan and had turned to go back to the house, lightening again became my foe and struck the very tree I was standing under. This time unlike before only a branch was damaged but nevertheless it came down, ripped away from the main trunk and landing exactly where I had just been standing. Needless to say I went home with great haste.

The third memory of this year that I have came in the August one month to the day of my parents wedding anniversary. It involved the death of one of our cats, Sandy. She died peacefully and was found by my mother in the morning under the chair in the kitchen where she always slept. A beautiful, as her name would suggest, sandy coloured Persian, she was not however, the most lovable of cats and her claws were the most formidable of weapons. Twice a year she would have to go to the vets to be shaved. A drastic measure but none the less a necessary one as her coat would become so matted that things began to live in it. Combing her was impossible and the wounds that we received from just trying to pick her up were proof of this. Her passing saddened me and I mention this only for one reason. About a week after her death I came downstairs before breakfast and after making myself a cup of tea I saw her quite happily sitting in our back garden enjoying the early morning sunshine and regarding the blackbirds with, unusually for her, peaceful indifference.

'Sandy' asleep in front of our lounge fire long after it had gone out!

Chapter 3 - 1979

When I compare myself as a nine going on ten year old child to children of the same age today I realise how much society is stealing our children's childhoods. Back then I was still very much a little girl and definitely not a nine going on nineteen year old as many girls seem to be now. I loved my dolls particularly my Sindy dolls and would spend many happy hours playing with her in our garden. From freshly mown grass I would make her large open-plan homes and spend summer afternoons in imaginative play.

My other hobbies when I was not at school revolved around the islands and the lock. I loved fishing and would spend hours sitting patiently by the rod at various locations trying to catch that 'big one.' I knew every fish on sight by breed name and my only reservation was the fear of catching a river shark, or more commonly called a Pike. I had often seen this species either swimming in the cut or at the end of a fisherman's line and their size, particularly their teeth size did not warm me to them. Thirty-six to forty pounders were not uncommon and in the wrong hands even out of the water they were a formidable adversary.

My 'big one' was caught that summer one day in early June. I had gone fishing over at Hedsor Wharf which was then a private patch of river on the far side of the island and belonged to the Rowland family. Although it was private our family had been given permission to fish there many years before and it was a stunning and tranquil part of the river. The Rowlands lived on the mainland and access to them from our island was over some large stepping stones to a very small island and then over a bridge and up the private towing path to their house. It was on these stepping stones that I chose this particular day to fish.

Here the river was very shallow and only navigable by kayak or something similar and in the summer months it was easy to wade out some distance before the water became too deep. It was also in this vicinity that you might be lucky enough to observe the salmon heading up stream to spawn, a pike taking an innocent duckling as a mid-afternoon snack or shoals of tench, trout and bream sunbathing in the shallows. On this particular afternoon all I saw was the sun shimmering on the crystal clear water and a kingfisher diving in and retrieving a bleak.

I had cast my line deep in the centre of the stream and had let it travel in the current until the swirls of water had brought it back within a few feet of me. I had repeated this countless times all afternoon with absolutely no success and was almost about to call it a day when I noticed my rod begin to bend. I began to reel in very slowly, noticing the pull of the line and the erratic movements of the float as it dipped and dived beneath the surface of the water. It was not long before the fish came into view and my, what a fish!   It was far too big for the hook and how it did not manage to break free I shall never know. I was never one for nets and I kept my tackle minimal. As I brought the fish in closer I knew that this was one that needed to be weighed and resting the rod against a stepping stone I reached down and picked up the fish. It was a tench and wow what a tench! I hung it on the scales and watched with excitement as the weight of the fish pulled the marker down past the 1lb, past the 2lb and on towards the 3lb. Tench never weigh this much and I could not wait to tell my dad.

Taking the hook from its mouth I wished it a happy life and returned it back to its home. I then packed up my equipment and ran back to the lock. "Dad!" I yelled catching him up by the lock office. "Dad, I caught a tench, 3lb 5ozs!"
"Well, where is it?" he asked.
I looked at him with complete ignorance and replied "I put it back of course."
He looked at me, shook his head and walked off. Now completely confused and feeling more deflated by the second I ran after him to find out what I had done wrong. It turned out that if I had kept it or photographed it I would have had the proof required to put both the fish and me in the record books. The average weight of a tench is just 2lbs. You live and learn.

One of my fish that did not get away!

The episode of the giant tench was to be the start of a good summer. It was the year of my parents twenty-fifth wedding anniversary, it was the year that I changed schools as the Convent became a college, it was the year that I became more involved in running the lock and it was the year that I definitely saw my first ghost.

I say definitely because there was another incident that occurred which to this day still leaves me perplexed and with no rational explanation. On summer days when I had nothing better to do I often went over to play with Mr and Mrs Rowland's children. Mostly they would call my father on the telephone and ask if I wanted to spend time with them or they would simply just wander over and see what I was up to. One day my dad told me that they had rung and I happily left our home and went over. I say happily because not only did I enjoy our games and their company but I loved their grand home. Both Tiny and Rosemary always made me very welcome and within their home I can honestly say that I had the best games of hide and seek ever!   On this particular day I remember it was a gloriously sunny with not a cloud in sight and with the sun beating down, birds singing in the trees and the feel of fresh grass beneath my feet I half skipped half sauntered my way across the island.

Towards the far side of the island there is a steep, grassy bank which then flattens out before it again drops away to the river. As I approached the bank I was in full skipping mode and did not realize I was upon it until it was too late. Like tumble weed I rolled head over feet and came to rest somewhat shocked half way down the bank breathing heavily and trying not to cry. I pushed myself up and as I rubbed my grazed knee something beside me caught my attention. I had come to rest beside what I first thought was a large stone or boulder but as the pair of black, eyeless sockets stared back at me I knew I was wrong. Lying right beside me, half submerged in the soil and grass was a skull and as I stared at it in horror realization dawned that it was human. I prodded at it with a stick that was lying close to me and this caused it to dislodge slightly. The sudden, unexpected movement caused me to jump and now quite frightened by what I had discovered I picked myself up and ran without stopping all the way to the Rowland's house. Telling the children of my discovery we decided to go back and investigate.

We all trooped off and after several minutes arrived back at where I thought I had fallen. We searched the area with almost fingertip detail for quite some time, possibly even as long as an hour but there was no sign of the skull, human or otherwise. I was completely confused. I was positive that I knew where this had happened but there was not even the evidence of flattened grass where I had slipped down. Eventually and somewhat bemusedly we left the island and went back to their home. To this day I still do not understand what had happened. If I imagined the incident then I must have imagined falling down but the graze and grass stains on my knee proved otherwise. The simple truth is I do not know.

Back at home my dad decided that it was time that I worked out on the lock-side and I soon discovered that I relished assisting my father on the lock. I began helping out because my father saw it as a means to stop me from being bored during the summer holidays. My relationship with my father when indoors was not that good. I was not the tidiest of children and he would nag my incessantly over the state of my bedroom and anything else that he could find fault with. Standing up straight, not interrupting during a conversation, never using the word 'can't' and speaking correctly were particular favourites of his irks with me. Since my brother's death his nagging and constant reprimanding had increased ten fold and looking back now I realise how much stress my mother had to endure.

However, working with my dad on the lock was completely different. We made a fabulous team and he taught me so much that it was not long before, even at that young age I was more than capable of running the lock single handed and often covered for him especially first thing in the morning when he was out collecting the fresh milk and bread for the shop. I never saw working on the lock as a job even in later years when I was actually employed as weekend assistant, summer assistant and then relief lockkeeper. It was fun, even when the weather was atrocious, the boaters were foul mouthed and the tragedies struck.

Running a lock looks easy - but it isn't, not always. It takes constant observation, an immense attention to detail, a crucial knowledge of volume, area, boat size and weight and the patience of a saint! Cookham Lock is just over one hundred and eighty-two feet long, twenty-five feet wide and has a fall of just over four feet. Now the boats that travel through it range from kayaks, skiffs, and rowing boats that are approximately six feet long, a couple of feet wide and weigh no more than one hundred and ten pounds to steamers with a steel hull, a length of over one hundred feet and a weight in excess of one hundred and thirty tons. With this variety of vessels in a small area at any one time common sense is a must. Running the lock was a little bit like fitting a jigsaw together with the only difference that if the wrong 'piece' was slotted in the results could be devastating.

Now days a good summer on the Thames is considered to be logging two thousand boats in a season, back then we could easily do five to six times as many! From nine in the morning to seven at night when dad was supposed to finish but very rarely did, all you could see were boats. They were moored up top and bottom of the lock waiting often over two hours to come in, and when mooring became non existent they would be queued up round the bend and well out of sight in either direction.

The first problem was bringing them in safely and in order. It sounds easy but when you have hire boats and the skippers have only handled a boat for less than an hour the scene can change in seconds from a tranquil river view to that of bumper-cars in a fairground. Boats are not cars, they do not react as quickly as cars and so over steering them was common place. We would have to make sure that no one missed their turn in the lock but it was sensible to bring the novices in first so that they would not cause damage to the private boats. Often the private boat owners did not appreciate this and we would spend many minutes calming down irate boat owners (usually those with the biggest boats) who could or more than likely would not understand why they were not first in the lock when they were first in the queue.

Passenger steamers were one of the challenges that we would face. Twice daily, usually around ten-thirty in the morning and then around tea time they would arrive at the lock. These were owned by Salters Steamers who ran daily sightseeing trips between Marlow and Windsor taking paying sightseers down and then upstream for a day trip. These were what we classed as 'real' boats. Steel hulled, handsome Goliaths licensed to carry over a hundred people (depending on which boat) and these, also much to the annoyance of private boat owners also had preferential treatment. The reason for this was two-fold, firstly because they were working vessels and secondly because of their size it was best to get them out of the way.

I can remember on one occasion when we let one of these boats in ahead of several others and a gentleman was most aggrieved to the point where he came up and decided to question me vociferously about it. My father knew I was more than capable of holding my ground, let me get on with it and as this man screamed abuse at me I became aware that something was not quite right with the steamer. It was coming into the lock far too fast and the skipper was looking concerned. Ignoring the gentleman's ranting I signalled to dad and watched helplessly as the steamer came to a stop only because of the head lock gates. There was an almighty crash and black, sooty smoke came billowing out from the steamer's engine. It turned out the steamer's throttle had stuck in forward and had there have been a boat in front of the steamer it would have been crushed to nothing but fibreglass flakes. I remember turning to the man and saying something like. "I'll put you in ahead of the steamer next time shall I? I am sure you must be insured for accidental damage?"

Once we had fitted the boats into the lock it was then a case of closing the gates, either lowering or increasing the water levels to the level above or below the lock gates. This was done hydraulically by either opening or closing the sluice gates within the lock gates and usually would be mishap free. The only problems would usually occur when the boats were travelling downstream and this was lovingly called a 'hang up.' This would happen after the boats had entered the lock and the crews had secured their boats to the bollards and switched the engines off. The problem came in the words securing their boats as many would treat this as a period when their boat would have stopped moving when in actual fact the boat would be lowering as the water was being let out. Of course one would want their boat to be going down with the water but if the boat had been tied off too tightly it would end up listing to one side as it caught on the edge of the lock. The most spectacular of these I witnessed was on a steamer. All the passengers who were Japanese tourists thought it was quite normal for them to be leaning so severely to one side to the point where they were sliding off their seats, and as no one was paying attention (the entire crew had gone up to mum's shop) we had to close the sluices down and refill the lock.

There was one job on the lock that I hated. Every so often we would have a 'Lock Inspection.' The locks in those days were run by the Thames Conservancy and the senior River members would like to see that their staff were, quite rightly, maintaining their locks to a high standard. They would travel the river aboard their rather plush vessel the 'Windrush' and inspect the locks for safety and presentation. Many of the locks had large gardens and ours was no exception. My task was to ensure that every blade of grass along the edges were regimental in length as the lawnmower could not be used right up to the concrete paths as it would ruin the blades. I had to do this laborious, back breaking task without missing so much as an inch because yes, my father would notice and it was not worth his wrath if I slacked on this. Like all lockkeepers then, my father was very proud of his lock and meticulous about its upkeep. Oh yes, my tool for this job - a pair of old, blunt, kitchen scissors!

I was not well in the July of that year. I had a severe bout of tonsillitis. It had started around the 10th of that month and had carried on for a good couple of weeks including through my parents wedding anniversary which was on the 17th.

Being ill in our house was never a lot of fun as you would be put to bed and told to shout if you needed anything. Shouting with tonsillitis was bad enough but with the walls of the house so thick no one would hear you anyway, so most of the time I lay in bed feeling sorry for myself with no company but my dolls and teddy bears.

One night, just prior to my parents' anniversary I woke up feeling incredibly hot and virtually unable to breathe. I tried to call out but no sound would come from my throat and so I just laid there in the dark crying in pain and feeling abandoned. I was not alone for long but what came terrified me to the point where somehow I managed to find my voice and scream for my mummy. Through my open window came spherical shaped lights. There were four or five of them and each were the size of a tennis ball. They glided in through the window and floated around my room, dancing round my ceiling light and hovering just about my head. They were the brightest and purest of white in colour but throbbing gently in amongst the white were gentle shades of purple, gold and blue. As soon as I started to scream they zipped out of the window at tremendous speed and never returned again.

My mother, woken by my screams ran into my room where through hysterical tears I told her that spaceships had visited me!   She assured me that this was not possible and said that they were probably car headlights and that I should try and get some sleep. Although I calmed down her explanation did not make sense and even today it still does not sit comfortably with me. You see, from my window my view was the lock. Beyond was Hedsor and then

Buckinghamshire but between these two points were Cliveden's woods and in summer the trees were thick with leaves. I admit that it may have been just possible to glimpse the odd, almost indistinct car headlight but not to the extent that I had seen. Also, a car's headlights are flat when they reflect on a surface and they only follow where the light hits. Light can only travel in straight lines so this cannot explain what I saw. The lights that came into my room were three dimensional, beautifully coloured spheres and travelled where outside reflections could not have reached. To this day I do not know what they were (although I now believe that they may have been 'spirit orbs') I am convinced however, that they were not reflections and not anything else that could have been caused by our natural and *normal* world.

My parent's wedding anniversary party was held on a steamer and was considered to be a great success. Family and friends mixed easily with each other and my mother's choice of apparel was a large and positive talking point. She had worn a made to measure sumptuous pink sari and she really did look quite beautiful, the belle of the ball in fact. I on the other hand happily played the role of the 'shrinking violet!' I still felt awful and the photos taken on that happy evening more than show this. It was several days before I was back to my old self again but was then fully able to enjoy my summer holiday. It was the following month when the next strange occurrence confronted me and again this took place in my bedroom.

My father was a stickler for me being in bed the same time every night barring special occasions and of course Blake's Seven! Bedtime for me was seven-thirty and in the summer I found it particularly hard to sleep. When I couldn't sleep I read and in the summer with the long, light evenings this was easy to do without being caught. (Reading during the winter evenings was far more difficult to achieve and I often resulted to reading under my duvet with the help from a torch.) One evening in August I was reading in bed. It was way past my bedtime but still very light. I was entranced in one of those Girls Annuals, 'Mandy' or 'Jinty' I believe it was called and I was completely engrossed in a story about an unusually coloured daffodil. I was lying on my side with the large, hard-backed book propped up in front of me when I thought my eyes had started to water. I rubbed my eyes to remove the tears but there weren't any. I then realised that if my eyes had been crying the words on the page would have been blurred but they weren't. It was beyond my vision of the book that was fuzzy. It was as if my room had filled with water or that is what it seemed I was looking through.

Lowering my book to readjust my vision I immediately became aware of a pair of legs standing in front of me right by the side of my bed. Slowly, I followed the legs upwards and found to my surprise a figure of a man standing directly in front of me. He was dressed in Tudor apparel and either I was seeing him in sepia or his clothes were mainly brown in colour. He was well dressed and maturity now tells me that maybe he was a merchant or someone of similar standing. He had a perfectly trimmed beard, the most sparkling blue eyes and he even had a cloth cap perched on his head.
What struck me most was the look on his face as our eyes met. I do not know who was the most astonished to see one another although I think if I am honest he was far more amazed to see me than I see him. He had a look of incomprehensible surprise almost as if this was not the place in the Universe or ether he was expecting to be and I am positive that the last thing he presumed to find when he appeared in my bedroom was me.

Within a couple of seconds of our eyes meeting he began to vanish before me and even his vanishing was odd. The only way I can explain it is to give you the image of standing on a bridge and throwing a fairly large stone into deep, crystal clear water below. Although the stone falls further and further away becoming more and more blurred as it sinks eventually into the blackness you are still standing in beautiful daylight. And that is as close as I can describe it but instead of him sinking downwards he drifted backwards getting smaller and smaller surrounded by a shimmering, watery-like mist. The peculiar thing was that he did not drift backwards in our time because if he had, he would have ended up going through my bedroom wall, into my parents' bedroom and then downstream! It all took place within his mist. It was as if I witnessed him backing through a doorway to another World.

I suppose I should have been scared but fear did not enter me that

34

evening. I admit I was slightly dumbstruck but I just picked up my book and began reading again almost as if it never happened. After a few minutes I laid the book on the floor and gave the incident my full attention. The conclusion I came to was that I had just witnessed something incredibly special.

The rest of the year I suppose could have been classed as a spiritual disappointment. An odd but perfectly explainable experience occurred on my first day of my new school. I had not visited the school before the September (or so I thought) and so on my first day I had quite a shock. Halidon House School for Girls was set amongst the sprawling natural beauty in an area of Fulmer near Slough. Unlike Slough it was a mainly rural area and the school itself rested in glorious surroundings. Huge lawns complete with tennis courts drifted down into a woodland area and all embraced an old, beautiful building. The entrance to this building came off a turning from the main road. A long, winding drive flounced down to the main entrance which was almost stately in its elegance. In front of the main entrance hall a circular pond complete with fountain greeted its visitors and it was a vision that was not easily forgotten. So true is this statement that when my parents took me in on my first day the strongest feeling of déjà vu swept over me to the point where it made me feel quite nauseous. I was positive that I had never been to the school before but if that was the case then how come I recognised it? The explanation came from my father who informed me that while he was coach driving one of his jobs involved the Halidon school run and I, although I had no recollection of it, accompanied him on several occasions.

Back at home the nagging from my father increased as did the bullying from my brother. There was one saving grace and that came in the form of David's girlfriend Shirley. Between his work and seeing her it meant that I saw less of him, something I was very thankful to her for. Looking back at the nagging that I received from my father one element of it was very unfair. As the nights drew in I was forever being told off for leaving my bedroom light on when I had left the room. I knew I had turned the light off as I wasn't a glutton for punishment from my dad but I couldn't prove it. It was only in the following years that I realise that this was indeed the start of the poltergeist type activity that eventually became part of my daily cycle of living with the ghosts of Cookham lock.

Chapter 4 - 1980

1980 did not start off too well for me. On the last day of 1979 my parents left for a three week holiday to Australia - without me! I spent those weeks in the care of my Godparents and in truth I made their life hell! I missed my mother dreadfully and that played a large part of my reasons for misbehaving. I cried almost all the time, had temper tantrums for no reason, said the most horrible things to them and generally acted like the proverbial spoilt brat! Also, the fact that I did not understand why my parents did not take me with them and why I could not stay at home with my brother (the fact that we would have probably killed each other was immaterial) played a part in my atrocious behaviour. So looking back I could not honestly say who was more pleased to see my mum and dad - me or my Godparents!

Although I keep repeating how much I loathed my brother there must have been some love buried deep within me for him because in the March of that year whilst he and his girlfriend were out on his beloved Triumph motorbike he was involved in an accident. Thankfully neither of them were hurt but they were both extremely shaken up and seeing them come home with ashen faces and the fear still in Shirley's eyes made me come to a rather touching decision. I decided that I would save my pocket money for him so that he could purchase another bike! Whether he knew this or not I do not know but on only fifty pence a week I am glad he did not rely on my meagre income for his next purchase.

I remember very little of this year, primarily just the main events but an incident that happened at school is worth mentioning. In the July of that year I came first in an English exam at school and this meant much to my friends' annoyance that the school put me up into the next class.

It was a warm summer and many of the lessons were taught outside under the shade of an enormous pine tree. Here we often sat during our lunch break when we weren't sunbathing and it was here that I learned that the school was haunted! There were supposedly various ghosts that occupied the sleeping quarters upstairs but to my interest there was a ghost that was in the vicinity of the old pavilion. This building was a very ornate, small wooden structure that sat close the edge of the playing field. I was told that quite recently two older girls had sneaked into the building one night and had messed around with an Ouija Board and since then strange things had happened. What the strange things were I can't remember but a school friend and I decided it was worth investigating. Although what happened was more than likely kids mucking around the fact that I couldn't find these 'kids' left me very unnerved after the incident.

During a lunch break we went into the building and began quietly calling out to any ghosts that may have been hiding in there. Almost immediately a few small pebbles came clattering down from the roof. I ran out immediately but there was no one around. I went back in and began calling out again. The same thing happened but with one major difference. This time a shower of stones came rolling down the roof and then one of the small panes in the window broke. No pebble came near it, the glass just shattered on its own. If that was not bad enough it was the shape that was left where the glass should have been that made us both scream out in fear and hastily leave the building. The hole in the glass looked exactly like the Devil's head. This may have been a classic case of pareidolia but whatever it was made sure that I didn't trespass in the Pavilion again.

The summer of that year was also very busy boating wise and in the early October my parents held a barbeque for all our friends and any boaters that wished to attend. For a small fee they received various typical grilled meats, I was in charge of the baked beans and my brother dished out the jacket potatoes. With Shirley helping as well we served a veritable feast to nearly 450 people!   With the help of a steamer moored up near the barbeque with an on board bar and disco a jolly time was had by all except my mother. The evening had started out well enough but in the early hours one of the revellers became a little too intoxicated and my mother went to see if he was ok. She caught up with him just above the lock near a very steep part of the river bank and although accidental, he swung round and she ended up rolling down the bank and landing inches from the river.

In the meantime an ambulance had been called for this drunken gentleman and so my father asked them to look at my mother's wrist which was extremely painful. The ambulance crew assured her it was not broken just badly sprained. My mum spent that night in agony and upon a visit to the hospital the following morning x-rays showed that her wrist was severely fractured and would need to be reset and kept in plaster for many weeks.

The gentleman who caused my mother's injury was needless to say very apologetic although he swore he could not remember any of those evenings' incidents. It turned out that what he had said was probably true as time proved him to be a very troubled man. He was an extremely intelligent man but his intelligence could not help him with his university religious studies and it was soon after this, maybe within a year or so that he took his own life. He was found hanging from the supports underneath Maidenhead Bridge.

Although I cannot find records of this in my mother's diaries I believe it may have been this year that we had a VIP come to stay with us. He stayed several months enjoying the main island which he immediately took to.

There was never a shortage of animals on the island. Our farmer, Stan Pope rented the island to graze his cattle, sheep, occasionally donkeys and of course my (his) two horses. In the year that my brother died I had been severely thrown from Miffy, a very rude and nasty mare. She had a mind of her own and was very flighty to say the least. On the particular day I had managed to get her to trot in the direction I had wanted her to go in without a lead reign. However, when I called my father over to show my achievement; with an exuberant cry of "Let's see what you can do," he had slapped her playfully on the rump and she had reared up and bucked. Unfortunately I was sitting on her at the time. She threw me off as if I was a rag doll and I landed head first on a rock. I suppose the hat that I was wearing at the time did save my life but nevertheless it split in two leaving my head to meet the rock at very close quarters. In those days my hair was down to my bottom and my father made me walk back to the house via the lock gates. The lock was full of boats and children on the boats nearest to me began screaming. It was not until my father rinsed my hair off in the bathroom that I realised why. My long blonde hair had turned crimson with blood and I must have looked like a victim from a horror movie. I received several stitches in my head from this episode and to this day have never been on a horse since.

Our VIP guest however was one horse I had no intention of getting too close to. 'Complacence' as I believe he was called was (so I was told) not only Redrum's brother but also the horse that was used for the Lloyds adverts on television. He was a majestic stallion who would run across the field leaping and bucking as if his very essence depended on it. He stayed with us for several months until one day someone came to collect him and it was the last we ever saw of him.

This celebrity was far from the only famous person/animal that I met during my time on the Thames. Most of the well-known faces that came through our lock (or used our islands for filming) did not really want to be recognised and certainly did not want the publicity that seems to accompany them everywhere now. I am not going to name drop but I did meet my fair share of actors, comedians, pop and rock stars, politicians and of course royalty. I can state however that thanks to my mother's instinct I did not become a victim to the late Jimmy Saville.   He arrived on the lock-side one day as part of a charity outing and my mother asked for his autograph for me. When he learned that I was ill in bed he said he would pop and see me as his visit would make me feel better.   Apparently he was most insistent but my mother categorically refused him an audience with me and for that I am eternally grateful.

There was however, one gentleman that I met and wished in latter years that I hadn't. He was staying with a friend of ours and when the friend brought him onto the lock-side I was introduced to him but told later not to mention that I had seen him. He was a dark skinned gentleman from the continent of Africa, very polite and well spoken. He later went into politics and I think the World, let alone the people of Zimbabwe regret the day he did.

I remember my birthday of that year with deep emotion. It was one of the very few times that I made my dad smile with pleasure and pride. We had to attend my school's annual prize giving and I did not want to go. It was my birthday after all. As I have already stated school was not my favourite place. I was only what could be classed as an average student. Although I excelled in English I struggled with the sciences, Maths being my particular nemesis and so I did not expect to win any prizes that evening.

So you can imagine my surprise when I was awarded the cup for the best student!   Halidon House School prided itself on teaching not just academic subjects but showing students how to behave in the outside world. Their instigations of courtesy, politeness and thinking of others were just as an important aspect as History, Physics and Chemistry. I will never forget my fathers face as I accepted the small, silver cup. I honestly believe that he was the proudest man on the planet at that moment.

The rest of the year was uneventful to my knowledge and with Christmas and New Year a quiet affair we moved smoothly into 1981.

Chapter 5 – 1981

This, as it turned out, was to be a year of emotions as assorted as any pick and mix bag of sweets that you could buy. The main family event of the year was to be my brother's marriage to Shirley but that was not due to happen until the May. Later in the year I had my first personal insight into adulthood with the start of my menstrual cycle. I mention this as there is a belief within Para psychological circles that girls who are undergoing this stage are more likely to suffer Poltergeist activity. Although it might explain this year it doesn't go to explain neither the many years before nor the greater years after, even to the present day. But maybe it explains why the entities in my home were gathering strength?

At the end of February that year I had been upstairs one evening reading in my bedroom. Even under my covers I had become too cold and had decided to go downstairs. After only taking a couple of steps I felt a heavy hand in the middle of my back and a second later I found myself lying at the bottom of the stairs in a crumpled heap with a grazed elbow, a twisted ankle and a bump on the head.

The sound of me crashing to the floor brought my mother to me where she gathered me up and with me limping badly led me into the lounge. Had she of arrived just a couple of seconds earlier she may of seen what I saw. On the landing, in only a loosely human form was a dark shadow. The mass was so dense that I could not see the wall behind it and as the lounge door opened so the apparition moved across the landing and into my bedroom. Needless to say I did not want to go to bed that night.

During the daylight hours I loved my bedroom but when the darkness came it was a different matter. I became convinced that I was being observed from the doorway and took to shutting my door up tight when it was bedtime. I took to always sleeping facing the door, just in case, you understand but I was never quite sure what it was just in case of. This sleeping habit has remained with me until the present day where I have always insisted in sleeping where I can see the bedroom door.

But it wasn't just the feeling of being watched. The room wasn't that big but at night it seemed as if the walls were moving in and I felt that if I were to stretch my hand out from under the covers then I would touch the far wall. The odd thing was I never had the confidence to find out. And then, there were the noises. The attic space although stretching across the whole of the roof was not that high and only possible to navigate if you were on all fours. So how come I could hear heavy footsteps almost marching above my head? We did have a large colony of Pipistrelle bats living in the attic and under the eves but unless they were wearing steel boots that would not explain the noises.

The other unexplainable situation was the continuing problem of my lights being left on even though I knew I had turned them off. In the July of this year my father lost his temper and we had a huge argument about it. I told him repeatedly that I was turning the lights off after I had left my bedroom but he refused to believe me accusing me of lying and being lazy. Did I think we had money to burn? The row left me in tears and also facing the conclusion that I was not being believed and if I wasn't being believed about something as simple as to who was turning the lights on, then my parents were certainly not going to believe anything else that was happening to me. This realisation confirmed my belief that I should not mention it again and for a couple of years I didn't. It was one night a few years later when something happened that made my father admit to the fact that maybe I wasn't lying after all.

The May of this year saw my brother marry Shirley. It was, as it should have been a happy and enjoyable event and a good time was had by all. I was thoroughly enjoying myself (even if I wasn't a bridesmaid) until the point where they came to leave late in the evening. When they came to say goodbye I suddenly got it into my head that I was loosing my brother. I had already lost one and I didn't want to lose another. Much to everyone's amazement I sobbed my heart out for the best part of an hour causing my brother to be kind to me for the first time in many years. Although I can truly say that we have only been great friends since my marriage in the year 2000 that was definitely the first step to reconciliation.

Since the death of Sandy in 1978 Spud, our aging tortoiseshell cat had been showing signs of her age. She used to belong to Neil but after his death we became inseparable and her tendency to sleep more and play less was beginning to worry me. As she was already twenty-three this year, most people would have said that this was more than normal and I should have been pleased with her great age but I didn't want to lose my friend just yet. Help was at hand. A relation of my Godparents had a cat that had just had kittens and we were asked if we would like one. I think it must have been fate as the kittens were born on my brothers wedding day and so on 27th of June my Godmother brought this tiny bundle down to the lock. Not caring whether this tabby kitten was a boy or a girl I had the name already sorted. I named him after my brother and sister-in-law as this seemed to be the most appropriate and so Sheda (SH for Shirley and DA for David) was welcomed into our family. Spud however, didn't welcome him. She was fast asleep on my father's chair when we carried him in and as soon as she saw him she gave the most malicious hiss I had ever heard come out of her mouth and shot out of the lounge in hasty disgust. It took a good couple of weeks for her to be in the same room as him and they frequently showed their loathing of each other - or so we thought. One evening when they thought we couldn't see them we found them cuddled up together and they remained the best of friends for several years to come. My plan had worked. Her life was rejuvenated and her playful and hunting skills were honed back up to what they had been just a few short months before.

Tiny our St Bernard, on the other hand was now giving us cause for concern. Now aged five he seemed to be acting much older than his still relatively young years.

A not so very 'Tiny' with me aged about eight

He hardly played and seemed to spend most of his time sleeping under the Yew tree outside our house. He was also losing weight and trips to the vets were proving inconclusive. In early November he developed a cough and a few days later he was readmitted to the vets for more in-depth tests. On the evening of the 18th we went to collect him but when my mum came out of the vets without him I knew the worst. He had been diagnosed with lung cancer and had been given just two weeks to live. Not wanting him to suffer anymore my mother said her goodbyes to him then and the vet put him to sleep. One of the last physical links to my brother had been cruelly taken away from us and for several weeks the house seemed empty and lifeless. How could an animal that spent almost all of his life outside in the fresh, clean, country air and never smoke, develop lung cancer? The cats missed him as well but little did we know that plans were already in motion and soon a new St Bernard puppy would be coming to live with us.

Several weeks later just before Christmas heavy snow arrived giving my father plenty of weir work to attend to and making the house feel colder than usual. Early one morning the cold woke me and the need to use the toilet was urgent. Entering the kitchen I headed straight for the bathroom and relieved myself. My urgent rush for the loo had woken the dog and as I headed back to bed I told him to go back to sleep. Obediently he lay back down under the kitchen table and it wasn't until I was warmly tucked up in my bed that I realised what had just happened. Oh how I wished I could have stroked my Tiny just one last time.

As far as my childhood goes 1982 was by far the best year especially the spring and summer although the year began very well. I had gone to stay with my best friend for the weekend and upon returning home on a dark Sunday evening I was greeted with a smallish bundle of soft brown and white fur belonging to a four month old St Bernard puppy. When I arrived home he was sitting on my mother's knee and in his joy at seeing me he had rolled off and came lolloping over to me, tail wagging as if he had only just discovered what it was for. My mother left the room immediately and moments later returned in her dressing gown. When my father had pulled up in the car after collecting me, apparently my mum had said to the puppy "Rachel's home." Even though he had never seen me before just the mention of my name had made him so excitable that in his anticipation to see me he had weed on my mother! The kennels' had nicknamed him Dozy and probably due to laziness on our part (and the fact that it suited him) his name never changed.

Dozy and I became the greatest of friends. If I went anywhere on the islands he came too. Apparently, at around four in the afternoon every weekday when I was at school he would disappear only to reappear with me when I walked home from school. When asked where I had found him I replied that he was just waiting at the weir gates. It soon became apparent that he was waiting for me.

He was a dog that loved to play and although he enjoyed a game of ball like most dogs his penchant on the toy front was for the smellier kind. He particularly liked cow pooh but his real favourite, his (in his opinion) crème de la crème of dog toys were fish!

One Saturday afternoon he discovered the small bay near the weir. It was very shallow and very good for cooling down hot St Bernard dogs. It was also very good for washing up bits of driftwood, tennis balls, drowned hedgehogs and dead fish! There are two smells I despise, one is the smell of gone off milk and the other is rotting fish. Dozy found the latter. Once it had been a rather large (maybe twenty pound or so) mirror carp but when our lovely, just washed St Bernard found it, it had probably been on the shore line for about two days. Two days in warm spring sunshine had not only made it nice and ripe but also slightly overcooked! Dozy thought it was perfect. He could shake it, roll in it, play pounce with it and generally have as much fun as a nine month old, long-haired St Bernard could. He just couldn't understand why he was not allowed in the house for several days and even with several baths people shied away from him if he went up to see them!

Early one murky evening I decided to take a walk up into the paddock. There was a thin mist lying low over the grass giving the lock-side a slightly mysterious feel and reaching for my coat I called the dog that was asleep in the lounge to take him with me. We had gone no further than the just outside the front door when a movement on the other side of the lock caught my attention. I could hardly believe what I was seeing. I saw travelling along the path, from the top of the lock towards the island what appeared to be a young woman. She was moving quite fast and seemed to be dressed in a long, light coloured gown. It was an unnerving sight because although she was moving quite fast she did not appear to be running or even walking at a quick pace. It was as if she was gliding. Her dress did not reach the ground as I could see quite clearly the path beneath where her feet should have been. With growing apprehension I realized that I could not see her feet at all. As she moved towards the gate that separated the lock from the island she seemed to fade away and never actually got to the gate at all. I was mystified not to mention slightly scared and decided that maybe a walk was not what I needed after all.

The following week dad decided that we should all go out for a meal and straight after he finished work we showered and changed and left just after six o'clock. We went to our usual restaurant that we frequented in Bracknell near Reading and after a very pleasant meal returned home close to eleven that night. As we pulled into the driveway my father got out of the car and said something like "What the bloody hell?" He pointed to the other side of the lock whereupon we all saw a figure running along the lock-side. It was a woman dressed in what appeared to be a long, white robe. The apparition was almost identical to what I had witnessed the previous week and the strong feeling of déjà a vu left me feeling sick and slightly faint.

As the woman disappeared into the dark my dad turned to us and was just about to say something when our attention was drawn to a pair of car headlights that were coming over the weir. Within a minute a police car drew up and two of our local police exited. He asked if we had seen anything strange and we enthusiastically regaled what we had all just seen. The policeman happily informed us that we had not seen a ghost but she was in fact a mental patient who had escaped from a secure unit, stolen a boat in Maidenhead and had been seen heading this way. The two policemen returned to their car and drove up to the entrance to the island to see if they could find her.

I never knew if they caught her on the island or if she managed to get over Cookham weir but I do know that she was eventually safely returned to the hospital where she had come from. What I found most disturbing was the fact that I had seen a premonition of this event the week before and could find no explanation for it. I wondered if I had caught a glimpse of the future but with everything paranormal that happened to me whilst living at the lock I have often asked myself whether it was me or the lock that was haunted.

It was not long after this strange event when we left spring behind and welcomed in the summer. The days were warm and the river was busy with boaters and wildlife. It is surprising what you take for granted when you are a child and the relationship I had with the local wildlife was no exception. What I thought was normal animal behaviour I much later, discovered was extremely unusual. From about the age of eight I was forever bringing injured animals home to look after and if I wasn't bringing them home they were coming to find me. I remember a pair of mallards that, after I had fed them a couple of times in the lock cut, sussed out where I lived and decided that it was far easier to have breakfast with me in our home than it was to go looking for it themselves. Feeding two ducks was not a problem but they must have told their friends about me because as the days wore on the ducks grew in number and after a couple of weeks it seemed as if we were feeding a small flock!

A pair of Mallards waiting for their Breakfast!

Then there was the swan incident. Every year a pair of swans nested at the back of our island in the weir stream amongst the reeds and marshy area. After several days of keeping an eye on them I had noted that the hen had a large clutch of eggs - I seem to remember at least nine or ten eggs and so I decided to see if some extra grain and bread would help her and her cob keep up their energy levels. They seemed very grateful for their additional food and would take it in turns to leave the nest for the extra I provided.

One day I forgot to feed them. Something must have cropped up - I can't remember what but after whatever it was I decided to lay on the lock-side and sunbathe. I had been laying there quite a while and was drifting in and out of sleep when I felt this sudden and aggressive shake to my foot. I sat up immediately to discover that the cob had got bored of waiting for me and had swam round the island and into the lock. My father later told me that he had watched the swan get out of the lock, walk up the steps and start looking for me. Apparently it had even checked the lock office before spying me and deliberately walking up the lock-side, crossing the top gates and walking down to where I was laying. My father said he watched in amazement as the swan had come quite close to my face and must have realised that I was asleep and so it had reached down and deliberately grabbed my big toe and shook it vigorously. Needless to say the pair had extra bread and grain as an apology!

What happened a little later in that summer was apparently even more astounding?   To me when it happened, it was just a lovely experience but according to an animal behaviourist that I found myself chatting with in recent years this sort of thing just doesn't happen. But I don't think it is unique, I just think that people do not always tell their experiences for fear or ridicule or being accused of lying.

It was July, about four in the afternoon and I remember it was a Sunday. I had gone for a walk around the large island and was parallel with the lock when something in the back water that led to Hedsor Wharf caught my eye. Here, the river was too shallow for any motor boats and so the wildlife held court. It was not unusual to see large fish here but it was the first time I had seen salmon. I watched in quiet amazement as a large shoal swam up river determined and forthright in their manoeuvres. I have no idea how many there were but I was mesmerized as they criss-crossed in and out, passing each other so, so close but never once touching each other.

As the last of them disappeared, heading for the weir I thought I had had my share of sights for that day but then something else caught my eye. A female mallard was swimming downstream quite close to the reeds and as I watched I noticed that she had babies. Ducklings are one of the cutest of baby animals and so I sat down quite close to the bank and watched as they swam by. But they just kept on coming. Now I don't know what the record is for the largest brood of mallard ducklings but I think I may have seen it then. Twenty-six, gold and brown, downy feathered bundles of trouble darted in and out of the reeds, zigzagging their mother to the point where I am sure she must have wished she was an owl and could turn her head in the same vein. How she had kept that many was beyond me. Even staying away from the boat propellers she had to avoid the pike who liked nothing more than a delicious young duckling to snack on.

I remember saying something to her along the lines of 'you've got your work cut out there' but I didn't think she heard me because she was too busy trying to keep them all together. I watched her pass me, heading downstream towards the main thorough fare and I was not surprised when she returned about five minutes later. The lock had just let out another full load of boats and I expect she preferred the peace and quiet of this back water without the worry of large and small boats potentially splitting up her family as they roared off down to the next lock. Again as she passed, I spoke to her and this time I think I said something to the effect of 'You must be shattered looking after this many babies' and to my surprise she stopped in mid-paddle and looked at me. A few seconds later she was calling her brood to her and directing them out of the water. They alighted only ten feet or so away from me and began charging in and out of the grasses, chasing flies and nibbling at bits of weed. Aware of the fact I was sitting up and must have looked enormous to them I laid down on my side, propping my head on my hand. To my astonishment mother duck waddled up to me and sat down within inches of me. Her brood followed suit except that they didn't sit down - well not at first. Nervously they came over and before long all twenty-six were using me as a playground!   They ran up and down my body, nibbling at my hair, tugging at my ears and clothes, jumping off my legs and shoulders and scrambling back up again for over half an hour and while all this was going on, their mother slept. Eventually mummy duck awoke, stood up, stretched and shook her wings, quacked gently to her brood and headed back to the river. Obediently her babies all followed her, some detouring on the way to grab a quick morsel, others almost racing her to the water. I watched them all swim back up stream and then quietly almost peacefully went home.

I saw the mallard and her brood several times after that. I was saddened to see that she lost three of her babies, but still looking after twenty-three what amounted to growing toddlers, and then to get them to adulthood in a dangerous environment was still no mean feat.

Where I became '*Nanny*' to the Ducklings! Also, above the bridge in the background is where I caught my 'big one!'

Chapter 7 - 1983

The beginning of this year gave me the proof that in one respect we treat animals far better that we treat humans. My father's mother had been unwell for some time and in the early part of this year she was diagnosed with cancer. My memories of her are vague and sadly incomplete. I remember she was a proud woman who believed that all young children should be seen and not heard. She was very strict and even after her husband's death many years before and her three sons leaving home she always kept herself and her home immaculate. She also made the best roast potatoes in the universe! As a youngster she used to terrify me but as I grew older she had more time for me and I began to understand and appreciate her much more. It was therefore sad that I did not get the opportunity to know her better.

Once the cancer had been diagnosed it was not long before, like a plague it spread and in a few short weeks it was in every major organ of her body. She was transferred from hospital to a hospice run by nuns and it was there that I last saw her.

I remember it being a cold and dismal place where everyone spoke in hushed whispers and the décor was drab and run down with paint peeling from the walls and a grimy substance smearing the window panes and blurring the view. The dying it seemed did not need interior design.

When we arrived at the hospice we were led to what seemed to be an endless ward and were told she was in the last bed on the left. We asked if this was true as the bed looked empty but we were assured that she was there. As we came close to the bed the nun was proved right but what was in that bed could hardly have been called my Gran. She was always a petite woman but what we saw was not much more that a skeleton covered with dead, flaking skin. Her hair was a mess and if she could have seen herself I know she would have been appalled to have been seen in such a dishevelled way. We were told that her passing was imminent and stayed with her for some time waiting for that final moment, but it was not to come. All of us were speechless when after a while she got herself out of bed and took herself off to the loo. After sometime we left her and returned home in sombre silence.

Excerpts from my mother's diary states that the doctor had given her only days to live but those days turned into weeks and it was agreed to bring her back to her home so that she could die in peace. But she didn't. Her stubborn will to live would not leave her and so the cancer just ate her up. She should have died weeks ago but instead she lay in her bed while the cancer pushed out her fingernails, split open her skin and flowed like an oil slick out of her wasted body. Apparently the doctor was so horrified that when he came to visit her he gave her an injection which put her into a coma. Had she have been a beloved pet she would have been put to sleep with dignity and kindness long before. She died a few days later.

Obviously this was not a good start to the year. For much of my Gran's demise I was left alone or passed between friends and family while my parents attended at my Gran's bedside. It was in truth a relief when the funeral was over and life returned to normal.

Spring soon arrived and with it the boats and the warm weather. I began helping out on the lock and also helping mum with the shop which was getting busy. In those days Environmental Health was not such an issue and so one of my jobs was baking cakes and making pies and pasties for the passing trade.

It was not long before I had another job. I became a mummy!   Now before anyone panics this was not to a human baby but to the small feathered variety. One afternoon my dad buzzed the house from the lock office and said that I had better get out there - he had something for me. Upon arriving on the lock-side I was handed a large box. "Bloody boaters thought it was lost," said dad. Looking inside the box I spied, tucked as far into the corner as it could get the tiniest of ducklings. It could have been no more than two days old. As I carried it gently back into the house my dad's words followed me. "Don't get too attached to it, it probably won't survive the night."

I took it indoors and gently picked it up out of the box and holding it carefully turned it over looking for any sign of injuries. It appeared to be unharmed and so I found some more bedding for it and made it comfortable. I then set about finding it some food and water. Remembering my dad's words I paid it little attention that day and just kept checking it from time to time.

The day wore on and the weather became heavy and humid. By nightfall it was obvious that we would be in for a thunder storm and so at the appointed hour I went off to bed taking the box and duckling with me knowing that it would be safer in my room behind a closed door and therefore out of reach of our kill-anything-that-moves cat!   At about midnight the storm broke and my word it was a humdinger! Now I love a good storm and for me the more thunder and lightning the better but my baby duckling was not so keen. In his box away from his mummy he cheeped and cried terrified at what he did not understand. My impartial stance towards him departed and feeling sorry for him in the end, I picked him up and brought him into bed with me. Immediately he snuggled down into the crease of my neck and with my hair falling gently over him like his mother's wing he fell asleep. Without realising it I too fell asleep.

It was not the warm spring sunshine that flooded in through my bedroom window that woke me that morning but the gentle tugging of my nose. Duckling was up and wanted breakfast. Placing him back in his box I went off to find some. In the kitchen I found my father.
"Morning daughter," he said. "I was about to bring you up a cup of tea."
"I'll take it up with me," I replied.
"How's the duckling," he asked
I looked at him and smiled. "Hungry," I said!
Breakfast for duckling that morning was bread soaked in water but when my father went out for the milk and bread for the shop that morning he came back not only with the aforementioned but also a sack full of duck meal that he had 'borrowed' from our local farmer. You could tell that duckling much preferred his lunch to his breakfast!

As it was our Easter Holidays I had plenty of time to teach duckling all he needed to know about being a duck and although he was very tiny the first thing he had to learn was how to swim. Now we all know the saying 'like a duck to water' so obviously teaching him how to swim would be no problem because he was, well, obviously a duck!

The plan was simple, I found my old baby bath filled it with water and placed it in the garden and then I fetched duckling and took him to his specially adapted toddler pool. Sitting down on the grass I made myself comfortable and with much anticipation I placed duckling into his pool. He hopped out so quickly you would have thought there were sharks in it! I put him in again and the same thing happened, in fact the same thing kept happening all afternoon until, feeling like a failure I gave up and went inside.

It seemed that being a parent was not as easy as one first thought and so with this in mind I asked my parents for some advice all of which I duly took. I poured out the water and used river water, I used river water with weed, I took him down to where the river was very shallow and placed him in there, I put him in our bath, I put him in the sink; my brother suggested trying him in the toilet (this advice I did not take) but to no avail. I came to the conclusion that I had the only duck in the world that could not swim!

Duckling and I were inseparable but as my holidays came to a close it was time to return to school. Now Mary might have had a little lamb that followed her to school but this was not an option for Duckling and so my mother agreed that while I was out during the day Duckling could have the run of the spare room. This worked fine although during my absence Duckling refused to eat and apparently just sat and sulked all day.

To start with we covered the floor with newspaper and made sure he had plenty to eat and drink and with the door closed he was safe from the cats. We had pale, cream walls in the spare room until Duckling moved in but Duckling must have thought that they were boring and for that matter so was the newspaper. He chose not to do his business on the paper but by aiming his bottom at various angles he discovered he could do the most wonderful and decorative v-shaped, brown splashes all over the walls! It was amazing that something so small could not only produce so much but also aim so high!

The days wore on and the only non-swimming duckling in the world was growing fast, faster in fact than the other ducklings on the river but while they were all getting some kind of colour to their feathers Duckling was still very brown and had still yet to get his full plumage. I then realised that we had automatically decided that Duckling was a Mallard. Reference books proved otherwise. He was no common Mallard Duck; he was a grand, soon to be very large, Muscovy duck!   His size proved to be one of his assets as it was not long before our 'kill-anything-that-moves' cat and he came nose to beak. What our cat was expecting I am not sure but I am positive he was not expecting to have his nose bitten by a toothless, smug Duckling!   Strangely enough the cat decided to review his strategy on 'kill-anything-that-moves' as he and Duckling ended up with some form of animal mutual respect and they both left each other alone.

During every spare minute I spent my time on the lock and messing about on various boats. The weather was warm and sunny and one particular late May Day I was so hot that as seven o'clock came we left the lock filled up and I jumped in. It was wonderfully refreshing and knowing that the first of the evening steamers would soon be arriving I decided to do a couple of lengths. As soon as I started swimming away the only non-swimming duckling in the world who was sitting on the lock-side watching me, started cheeping frantically and before I knew it he was racing across the water to get to me. As soon as he arrived he calmed down and began swimming alongside me. So that's how you teach a duck to swim, I realised!

I do not believe in teaching animals tricks but somehow without realizing it I taught Duckling to sing!   Now, anyone that knows me will tell you that I have a singing voice that can terrify the dead let alone the living but Duckling seemed to understand my lack of vocal prowess and decided to do something about it. I can't remember how it actually started but one day while I was humming he pushed his beak into my mouth and began to make soft quacking noises. The more I hummed or *'la-laarhd'* the more noises he made and

58

apparently it actually sounded although rather unusual, rather good. It became a kind of party trick that use to amuse and intrigue friends and family alike.

My summer holidays eventually came around and the next part of learning to be a duck was soon to be realised. He had (eventually) taken to swimming and could regularly be seen in the water but still in close vicinity to the lock and to me. However, teaching a duck to fly was a little more difficult for obvious reasons. I must confess I did try the running round the garden flapping my arms like a deranged ostrich but Duckling was not interested and personally I did not blame him. I took this problem up with a friend who was a deck hand on one of the steamers and he came up with an idea which we immediately tried out and thankfully worked.

'Duckling' before he was fully grown and below 'Wow,' what a handsome fowl!

Duckling was now fully grown and even if I do say so myself, a handsome fowl. He was large with beautiful green and white plumage and was a very proud bird. What I didn't realise that teaching him to fly would actually make him arrogant!

It was actually relatively easy teaching him to fly. I passed Duckling to my friend who stood at one end of the lock and I went to the other and then my friend simply let him go. In his desperation to get to me Duckling flapped his wings so hard that he took off and was with me in seconds. I tell you, you have never seen such a look of triumph in a bird's eyes!

And that was it. It became a game. Now that Duckling was fully grown he ate outside so he was always first to his feed bowl. He particularly loved it if we were on the other side of the lock together. I had to *walk* around the lock and over the gates to do his food while he simply flew directly to his food bowl. I constantly received this look of 'What took you so long?!"

It was not long before Duckling ventured further afield and on the 24th of July he went missing. The mixed emotions were confusing - I had lost my friend but I had saved an animal and let it go back to the wild. Although I was sad I was immensely proud.

That, I am pleased to say was not the end of the story. I spent the following weeks catching up with friends and family and by mid-August I was back home and quite happy. On the 24th of August one month precisely to the day Duckling had gone missing one of my best friends had come over and we had decided to go fishing on the far side of the far island. Can you possibly imagine my surprise and pleasure that when we walked onto the lock-side carrying our rods and bait who was waiting to meet us? Duckling looked stunning. He waddled over to me, quietly quacking excitedly and then flew onto my shoulder. We stayed with him all afternoon and all thoughts of fishing went out of the proverbial window!

By 7 o'clock he left us but it was not difficult to follow him. He had set up home on the mainland on a quiet secluded bank and he seemed very happy. Although he did not visit daily I could often see him and all it needed was for me to call to him over the river for him to come to me. I am so happy to say that he lived a long and fruitful life and judging by the ducklings I saw the following year I can almost guarantee he became a father.

Although Duckling took up a large part of my time and sometime energy there were other things going on in my life. As far as my family were concerned the most important was the urgent need to find me a new school. Halidon House School for girls closed at the end of the summer term leaving not a lot of time for them to find me somewhere else which, for a thirteen year old they unfortunately did.

Not being a lover of my school years this period only added to my detestation because my new school was vastly different. Although private, the classes were huge and the girls not very friendly. Although some of my friends transferred to this school it was not long before just the thought of going to school made me distressed and unwell. However, with the prospect of O'Levels coming up I had little choice but to knuckle down and get on with it.

Autumn came and with it the news that our beloved St Bernard had Hip Dysplasia. Although we could not afford the cost of an operation his insurance allowed us to keep him relatively pain free with a daily dose of various drugs. I remember my mum telling me that had it had not been for the insurance it would have cost us £96.00 a week.

Autumn rolled into winter and Christmas was only a few weeks away when news from abroad threw us all into turmoil. My uncle in Australia had died suddenly and my aunt had urgently requested my mum's presence. Christmas with just my dad was not a prospect I was looking forward to.

Chapter 8 – 1984

How or where we spent Christmas is virtually a mystery to me. Vague memory and my mother's diary seems to show that my father may have managed to get a flight out just before the festive season but either way I ended up under the care of my brother again. In truth neither of us relished this prospect and this was born out by the fact that I did not stay there for the whole of my parent's absence. Christmas was hard work on both sides and I was counting down the minutes let alone the days or weeks before my parents return and therefore my return to the river.

But in the mean time I had far worse to endure, the thought of which then and now still leaves me cold - Boarding School. I remember the journey to my prison like it was yesterday. I remember the cold, icy conditions, my sister-in-law driving and skidding in the frozen slush and the false, sickly smile of the teacher who greeted me. It was the start of three weeks of Hell and an experience I promised then and fulfilled that I would never impart on my future children.

I was told that I was lucky - I had my own room, privacy or so I thought. But within a few short hours I realised that this was all a ploy, a cunning plan to help me relax into my new temporary surroundings.

After the tearful farewells with my brother during which my pleadings of not to leave me in this God Forsaken place had gone unheard, I unpacked. Other than the necessities I had brought with me a few chosen knick-knacks from home including a couple of posters from my bedroom wall. In truth I was never really into posters except one that I owned of Tottenham Hotspur but had always felt that teenagers put up posters as part of their expressionism and so I felt compelled to follow suit. I had chosen a couple of large portrait style pictures from the, at the time 'in magazine' 'Smash Hits.' My father had allowed me to have them on my wall so I thought that they would be fine.

All was going well and once I had unpacked I went to join the other 'inmates' for dinner where I was taught a valuable lesson. Now had I have been shown how to eat with chopsticks or the correct way to prise snails from their shells may have proved useful but my valuable lesson for that evening at dinner was how to wipe a table down correctly without spilling crumbs upon the floor!   Needless to say I was not that impressed and departed back to my room as soon as possible.

As soon as I returned I was horrified to discover that I had been robbed. I had not been there one hour and already my privacy had been pushed aside and had left me feeling as if I had been caught on the toilet with my pants down. I was furious. What right had the other girls to come into my room without my permission, especially in my absence?   The knock on the door interrupting my angry mental rant answered my questions for me, although not in the way I had perceived.

There stood our seamstress teacher who always reminded me of an egg. It was not that she was shaped like an egg it was just that she was always expressionless. "In case you are wondering your pictures were not suitable," she explained. "One of the younger children may see them and be shall we say, confused by them."
"But why would one of the juniors be in my room," I questioned.
"They may just wander in," she said refusing to look me in the eye.
I almost exploded with rage "Why would they just wander in when this is meant to be my room?   Surely even at seven years old they know what privacy means?   I thought this is what this school taught - appreciating other people's values." And then I realised that no matter what I said I wouldn't win. "Leave me alone now; I want to go to bed."

Other than being desperate to get home I remember little more about boarding school. My mother's diary tells that on one evening I called Australia but found no one in. Apparently she returned the call and was told all was well. And so for three weeks I was left in a school that I hated and with people that I had nothing in common with and a feeling that all was not well at home. If I had known then what I discovered when I arrived home I would have up and left and walked the twenty miles back to the lock in my night clothes if necessary.

On February eleventh I was collected from school by my brother and taken to meet my parents at the airport. I remember nothing of this, none of the happy reunion or the drive home. I know I came home with my parents but where my brother and his wife went I also have no knowledge of. What I do remember is pulling up in the car in our driveway where all my fears were realised. My mother's description from her diary reports it as: *'Gee its cold, fast ride home. Dozy looks great - full of life, different for poor Spud, a pathetic weak sight, immediate decision she must be put down, she can't suffer. Jim took her in* (to the vets) *5pm.'*

The truth was that while my parents had been sunning themselves on the other side of the World and I had been held against my wishes in boarding school my poor, beloved cat had starved to near-death. While my parents had been away the Relief Lock-Keeper had been charged to look after the animals and had been told that if there were any problems he should call the vet. He didn't. We didn't see Spud at first, not until she crawled, dragging herself round from the back of the house after hearing my voice. She was, quite literally skin and bone. Her eyes were bulging and there was no sign of the tortoiseshell colours that made her coat so beautiful. She was covered in her own faeces, her voice box had broken and according to the vet who quickly put her out of her misery it seemed as if she had been hanging on for weeks waiting for my return. Her death came just days before her 26th birthday. The guilt surrounding her hideous demise remains with me until this day.

While my father was out my brother and Shirley returned and learning of our cat's demise David gave me the briefest of hugs before returning to his bullish self. A few minutes afterwards my father returned home telling me how peacefully she went. I was so pleased that she was at last out of pain and so did not mind the ordering around and instructions of making tea and coffee.

Tea making was done for ease in front of the kitchen window. This was primarily because our larder was directly to the right and this was where the milk was kept. The floor in front of the larder was the only part of the kitchen that was uncarpeted and where the cats, now just Sheda our remaining cat, was fed.

While my parents regaled stories of Australia and the flight home I busied myself making the beverages. As always when I was at home I was bare footed and thought nothing of walking on the cold, tiled floor to enter the larder. It was as I stepped out of the larder that I stood on the cat's tail causing her to mew. I felt her tail under my foot and hearing her mew I immediately stepped away and looked down but there was no sign of the cat and I knew exactly why.

Calmly I called into the lounge "Where is Sheda?"

"On the sofa asleep," came the reply

"How long has he been there?" I asked still keeping my voice level and light.

"Since we opened the door and he ran in," was the answer.

My emotions overwhelmed me and with the milk flying across the kitchen I collapsed onto the floor sobbing uncontrollably. My beautiful cat had come back to say goodbye and I had stood on her tail. I was mortified.

Sheda, our young tabby with Spud. This was taken just prior to my parent's holiday

****

It was the last Saturday in April, a lovely warm day I seem to remember and my mum and dad and I were sitting down to dinner in front of the television. It was quite a novelty as dad had actually finished work on time and for once we were all eating food that did not need to be reheated. We had just started our meal when there came a knock at the door.

"I don't bloody believe it." said my mum and she threw her knife and fork down in disgust. "Why can't we have just one meal in peace?"

"Don't worry I'll go," I said and I went to the door. On the doorstep I found a middle aged gentleman looking very white and visibly shaking. I listened to what he had to say and told him that I would investigate immediately. Knowing that it was the wrong time of the month for an April Fool I went back to my parents and said to dad in a confused but excited sort of way "There was a man at the door who said that the lock side is completely covered in blood. I'll go and see what he is on about." As I left the house dad's fork had still not reached his mouth.

Knowing that a little blood could go a long way I wandered onto the side of the lock to see what the man was going on about. It did not take me long to discover that he had in fact been underestimating the amount of blood. It was everywhere. Huge great pools of red, sticky liquid were polka-dotted all up and down the one side of the lock but as to the owner of the blood there was no sign. At that moment I could have been accused of catching flies as I just stood there with my mouth agape and my hands firmly on my hips. Was it murder? Was it some kind of sick joke? I distinctly remember muttering to myself "What the bloody hell?"

I went back into dad and told him what I had found. "What I do not understand is where it has all come from," I said as we both went back onto the lock side. Like me he too was perplexed and after shaking his head we both toured the whole of the lock looking both above and below for any sign of a body. We found no trace and always being the first for wanting to solve a conundrum I went to examine the pools of blood more closely.

The blood was very fresh but already in the late spring sunshine it was beginning to congeal. It was then that I found a clue. I noticed that a dotted trail of blood seemed to join each of the pools and upon further inspection I noticed that some of the pools edges were smudged as if someone or something had walked in them. Following the puddles of blood methodically I reached the bottom end of the lock and there I found my second clue.

I was just coming to the conclusion that some strange, unknown river creature had caught various animals, slaughtered them on the lock side and then dragged their bodies down into the murky depths when the last puddle gave up a foot print. I studied it closely. It certainly wasn't human, definitely animal shaped, and then it struck me. I knew who the footprint belonged to. But it didn't make any sense. I had seen the owner of the footprint not fifteen minutes before and he looked completely fine to me. In fact when I had walked passed him he had looked up at me and wagged his tail. I walked back to dad and told him that I thought I had solved the mystery.
"Great," he said. "Do I have to call the police or not?" he asked.
"No," I replied "But you may have to call the vets."

Dozy, our St Bernard was still laying by the side of the house in the shade where I had seen him a few minutes before. I called him to me and immediately he stood up and walked over to me his tail high and wagging, his joules drooling saliva and his back legs completely soaked in blood.
"Oh my God," I said and then to dad "you had better call mum."
Mum came out and examined him, I examined him and then dad examined him but for the life of us we couldn't work out where the blood had come from.
"It's no good," said mum. "We will have to hose him down and see if it will start the bleed again."
This we did but no more blood appeared and so while dad washed down the lock side with buckets of water from the river mum drove the dog to the vets.

In those days the vet was a personal friend of ours - a boat owner and so he was happy to open up the surgery to see our dog. But he too could find no wound on the dog sent him home with instructions that if it were to happen again we were to call him immediately. It did happen several times and it was sometime before a diagnosis could be made. The cause of the dog's blood loss was actually made by accident. Several days later someone happened to notice the dog having a wee and happened to notice that when the dog's penis was extended blood started to appear. He was immediately taken back to the vet where upon his final and conclusive diagnosis was made. It transpired that the dog that was obviously dozy by nature as well as by name had gone for a wee too close to a rose tree. Whilst cocking his leg, he had inadvertently caught his penis on a thorn which had ripped the shaft severely enough to need several stitches.

As my mum said to me when she finally brought the dog home from the vets "I do believe there is a moral to this somewhere!"

'Dozy' by name & dozy by nature!

* * * *

Summer arrived slowly that year. Heavy rain eventually gave way to a warm and beautiful summer and sunshine was the one thing that the Thames needed to bring the boats out onto the river. Shirley's sister Liz and I had become good friends and often during that year she would come and stay for a weekend. One of our favourite pastimes was sitting on the bank at the top of the lock and watching the boats travelling though the lock. I must confess at this point that this is not strictly true; we were not so much watching the boats but watching for any scantily clad, young, good looking males that would happen to pass by!   If we were not men watching we would spend the weekends shopping in Maidenhead or fishing or just hanging around. Pleasures were simple in those days!

Now one weekend in early August Liz came over and after spending a hectic day man watching we retired for an evening of listening to music and watching television. Although it is not recorded in my mum's diary, at some point earlier in the year my parents had provided me with a portable, colour television. Many children believe that it is their right to have a television in their bedroom. These days it is commonplace even for very young children to have this box placed at a strategic point in their room so that they can fall asleep to whatever they want. Back then it was a novelty. It also meant that my parents didn't have to suffer the 'rubbish' that I enjoyed.

So far that year with the exception of my cat's death, paranormally speaking it had been quiet in our home. The picture still moved of its own accord and items disappeared and then reappeared several days later but that was now as normal to me as brushing my hair and I had become almost au fait with it. The weekend in question was to change that and leave me with the realisation of two points. Firstly, not everything that looked paranormal was paranormal and secondly well, sometimes it was.

During that year a new American Sci-Fi program had come to our screens and with the demise of Blake's Seven 'V' I think it was called, had taken its place. The storyline was basically about an alien invasion on Earth where reptilian like creatures had come to our planet disguised as humans with evil intent. They pretended to be our friends but in truth they were our enemies. Now that evening Liz and I had stayed up and watched this along with a late night horror film before falling asleep, me in my bed and Liz fast asleep on the floor on a 'put-you-up.'

It sounds a cliché but that night something woke me up. I had no idea then or now what it was but whatever it was caused me to wake and sit bolt upright in bed. I looked around dazed but alert staring into the darkness but seeing nothing. All I could hear was the sound of the water trickling through a gap in the lock gates and the thump of my blood pounding in my head.

As my eyes became accustomed to the gloom I happened to glance down and what I saw froze my being to the core with terror. Although still warm from the cosiness of my bed, my back and shoulder became almost solid with the cold that fear brings and for a brief instant I lost the line that divides reality with imagination. As I looked down I saw looking up at me a huge pair of silver, oval shaped eyes. They didn't blink, they just stared and I stared back too afraid to move. Thoughts of giant, alien lizards filled my brain and all of a sudden the television program seemed far scarier and far more real.

After what seemed like hours but couldn't have been I slightly shifted my position in my bed but still the eyes glared at me and gaining a little confidence by their lack of movement I reached down under my bed and grabbed for my torch. As I switched it on I did not know whether to laugh or cry but realized that I had been holding my breath. Relaxing but still trembling I shone the light directly into Liz's face but she didn't flinch. I flicked the light on and off, pulled faces at her but to no avail. There was no reaction, she was definitely asleep. I couldn't believe it. A human that slept with their eyes open! I had never heard of such a thing but believe me she heard all about it the following morning when she woke up!

Liz left late afternoon on the Sunday and feeling rather weary I decided to lie on my bed and read. I cannot remember exactly what I was reading but knowing that my taste in those days was strictly Steven King or James Herbert it would have definitely been a novel by one or the other of these two great authors.

The weather was warm and sunny outside but the book was too good and so it was sometime before I realised that there was a noise in my bedroom. It was a soft sort of dragging noise and when I looked up the first time I heard it I could not see any reason for it. I carried on reading. It came again but still I could not work out what it was. This time I only pretended to read and about five minutes later the noise repeated itself and I was ready for it. Looking up I managed to gain its direction. It was coming from in front of me and slightly to the left. I laid the book down beside me and studied the area in depth.

The dominating feature was the wardrobe with the television on top. Not being the most tidy of people the wardrobe was in disarray with each of the drawers that were down one side, open at various amounts. Next to the television there was a collection of tapes and books and general clutter. The noise could have come from any one of those areas.

Then the noise came again and this time I saw its cause. The third drawer down moved open ever slightly, not even half an inch. I sat transfixed, not even daring to move and then realising that I was not breathing I exhaled still staring at the drawer. After a few minutes when nothing else had happened I did something that I had never done before. I spoke to it. Very quietly I asked "If you just opened my drawer do it again."   I waited but not for long. Less than a minute later the drawer moved again. I jumped up and pulled the drawer right out. There was nothing behind it, nothing but the back of the wardrobe. I pushed the drawer back in.
"Do it again," I asked. It did.
"Is it you that keeps turning my picture around?" Again it moved.
I decided to ask one last question, not because I was running out of questions but because I was beginning to lose my nerve.
"Do you want to do me harm?"   There was a long pause and I was just about to run out of the room screaming when a different drawer, the one directly below it, began to move again. This time it did not open but slowly closed itself shut. Not knowing what this meant as an answer I left. I hastily decided that now would be a very good time to go and finish my book out in the sunshine. That night I slept in my other room.

The following day I ventured once again into my bed-sit room nervous at what I might find but all was peaceful and as I had left it. Feeling brave, once again I called out to whoever had shared my room with me the day before but as to a reply, there was none. Bemused, I left the room and went downstairs and although afterwards I was always nervous and intrigued, nothing more happened for a while.

As with all school holidays the time went on and during August I swung between being bored, out with my friends and working on the lock. The weather turned slightly cloudy and there was concern that the August Bank Holiday would be a 'wash out.' It was not the case. The sun came out and so did the boats and Bank Holiday Monday was no exception. From before nine in the morning it was manic. The river was hardly visible such was the volume of traffic upon the not so smooth waters of the Thames and my father who was working that weekend barely got in the house before ten every night and he still had to let the passenger steamers through after that hour.

I do not know what it is about holiday makers and water but all thoughts of common sense seem to vanish when you put the two together and such was the case that Monday. People seemed to pay less attention to their own safety and were more intent in drinking too much alcohol and generally mucking about. Several people fell in, boats collided with each other because they were going too fast and not looking in the right direction and arguments between boat-owners were as frequent it seemed as each lock cycle.

On one occasion my father bellowed at a young lad who was heading over to my mum's shop, not to run. My father's voice was enough to put the fear of God into anyone and the effect on this lad was immediate although short lived. While the lad was at the shop my father and I were talking to his dad when the lad returned. He had completely forgotten my father's warning and came charging over the lock gates at full pelt and then ran down the bank to where we were standing at the lock edge. Unfortunately this boy's momentum was too great and he could not stop. He quite literally ran past us and into the water. I watched in amazement as he disappeared beneath the surface, ice cream still in hand whilst my father carried on talking. Then in the second as the boy rose to the surface my father reached down and grabbed him by his shirt collar and hauled him onto dry land. It all happened in no more than three seconds and as the lad stood there, dripping wet with a complete look of bewilderment on his face my father gave him the 'dressing down' of his life. I had been at the end of my father's lambasting on various occasions and it was not a nice place to be. However, I do not think the boy heard a thing my father said as he still seemed to be looking down at himself and wondering how on Earth he got this soaked!

The morning raced on and before I knew it lunch time was upon us and that was when all hell broke loose. It was actually a dog that did the breaking loose!   A rat looking, mangy, brown excuse for a dog escaped from a boat and terrorised the three hundred strong flock of sheep that were grazing on the main island. Terrified sheep ran for their lives in all directions. Several ran over the cattle bridge and in sad but true lemming style flung themselves to their death over the weir. Others hurtled up into the paddock, some went into our garden and several more went down into the undergrowth at the bottom end of our island. Three sheep ended up in the lock cut but were all rescued by obliging boat owners who pulled them out of the river and dumped them crudely on the island just above our house.

Whilst all this was going on my father put a telephone call out to the farmer and soon after he and several farm hands arrived to mop up the mess. The sheep were scattered over eighty acres of land and the farm hands had a hard job rounding them all up. Meanwhile, I had noticed that one of the three sheep that had gone for a swim was still lying where it had been left by the kindly boat owner. As I walked over to it I was just in time to see its eyes roll to the back of its head. "Oh no you don't," I bellowed at it and so began the battle of girl versus sheep.

People think that sheep are not the cleverest of creatures. They follow each other around often paying no heed to the danger they put themselves in until it is too late. Then, when they know death is imminent they just simply give up and die. I think that they are actually quite clever. They know that there is safety in numbers and why prolong the inevitable?   I however, on this occasion, was not about to let the inevitable happen.

"Oh no you don't," I bellowed running over to it, grabbing its head and shaking it from side to side. Briefly its eyes came back and looked at me before rolling back once again. And so it began. You cannot do mouth to mouth on a sheep. Nor can you do heart massage, particularly as this sheep had wool that was several inches thick and now completely sodden with water. I would never have found the heart and it would never have felt it. But it would feel something stronger and so I slapped it. Then I kicked it. Then I thumped it. Then I slapped it, kicked it, thumped it, kicked it, slapped it and thumped it some more. Now before you think about calling the RSPCA out on me bear in mind the make up of a fully grown, heavily woollen sheep. It takes a lot, an awful lot for them to feel something. Every time I thought I was getting somewhere and the sheep showed some response I would stop and then the sheep would give up so I started all over again. It seemed to go on forever.

Then at one point a farm hand walked passed me and I asked him where he was going. He said he was off to find the remainder of the flock that had been spotted huddled up at the far point of the bottom end of the island. I did not envy his job as if they were where he described, if they were startled again they would all end up in the open river and little could have been done to save them. It was at that point that I had a bit of a brain wave and asked the farm hand if, when he returned with the remaining sheep he could herd them past us. I watched him walk away and continued with my unusual but necessary sheep lifesaving technique.

I was rapidly coming to the conclusion that I was going to lose this fight as the sheep did not want to play ball. It seemed to have lost all interest in living and I was in truth now completely knackered. I had no idea how long I had been at it. A while later I heard the sound of bleating and looking up I saw a small flock of about ten sheep heading directly towards me. As they came closer I moved out of the way and let the flock run past. My sheep did not move. Then, the very last sheep to pass him stopped, turned round, came back a few paces, nuzzled him very briefly and gently on the nose and then trotted off with the rest of his mates. Immediately my sheep leapt up and ran after the others as fresh and new as a bloody spring lamb!   I didn't know whether to laugh or cry!

I stood there dripping in sweat and sheep grease whereupon I saw the farmer Stan Pope talking with the farm hand a hundred yards or so up the path. Stan finished his brief conversation with the young man and stomped down towards me. Stan was your traditional, original style farmer. Back then he was already in his late sixties and in all the years I knew him he never seemed to change. He was always dressed the same whenever I saw him tend his animals. He wore a brown suit, collar and tie, a filthy long Mack and equally filthy Wellington boots.

"You been working hard my dear so I hear?" he asked. I nodded, too tired and dry-throated to find my voice. He put his hand in his trouser pocket and pulled out a huge wad of twenty pound notes.

 "Saved that sheep's life I understand and saved me a fair few quid. I lost six of my darlings today but it could have been seven. I think I owe you this." and flicking the notes off the roll of money he handed me three twenty pound notes. I managed a heartfelt but husky 'thank you' before the pair of us walked down to my mum's shop whereupon he bought me an ice cream and a much needed can of shandy.

August soon rolled into September and with this month came the return back to school. It was to be the start of my two year study for O'Levels leading hopefully to go on to college to study Nursery Nursing. In truth this was not my ideal choice of career. I had planned to join the Thames Valley Police Cadets but they were to be disbanded and this left me in a quandary. Nursery Nursing seemed like a good second option because after all, I liked kids!

That September brought with it the autumnal glory that was, as always, fully justified by Cliveden's Hanging Woods. Their blaze of colour of reds, gold's, auburn, oranges and yellows was a natural spectacle that was too beautiful to even catch on canvas.

I had been back at school a couple of weeks and had settled into the new class fairly well. My weekends had been spent helping dad clear the leaves from the lock-side and lift the Dahlias out of the soil for the winter. There had been a few boats around but now as the season was rapidly drawing to a close it was the time to catch up on all those jobs that a busy season had prevented us from doing. So, on that third Sunday in September I had gone to bed tired from a busy weekend and with everything right in my world.

I do not know when my nightmare started or how long it had been going on for but it was so bad that it woke me with a fearful shudder and I found myself sitting bolt upright in bed. The good thing about nightmares is, that as soon as you wake up they are gone, over with, finished. You calm down and you go back to sleep. So imagine how I felt, when sitting up in bed I realised that my nightmare was continuing and I was wide awake? At first I struggled to work out where I was and confusion was getting the better of me and adding to my fear. The noise that I had head in my sleep had carried over into my waking and the flight or fright instinct that we all have took over and I buried myself under my covers. WHAT THE HELL was that noise?

Envisage if you can a pack of about thirty wolves fighting outside your bedroom window? Envisage if you can the sound of the howling, the snarling, the whining, and the frequent snap of their jaws; the growling, the barking and the tearing of flesh as they rip into each other or something else. That is the best way to describe what I could hear the only difference was there wasn't a pack of wolves outside my bedroom. Had there of been I would have heard their movement; the sound of their nails on the concrete, their bounding about and the sound of their thuds as they hurtled into each other. But what was worst was the realisation that all the sounds I could hear were coming from one voice box. It was as if the sounds were laid on top of each other fighting to be heard and the ventriloquist that was controlling them had been possessed.

I buried my head under my pillow and lay there too scared, too petrified to move. I now know the true meaning of being frozen in fear and found myself praying for the noise to end. But it didn't. It just went on and on. After about fifteen minutes I heard another sound and with it came the understanding that I wasn't going mad. My mother was also crying and my father was trying to comfort her.
"Dad," I called out "What is it?"
"I don't know," he replied "But stay where you are. Stay in bed. Whatever you do, do not go near the window. I repeat, do not look out the window."
"Are you going to find out what it is," I called back hoping for some reassurance?

"No bloody way" he said.

Now I knew I had reason to be scared. My father was frightened of nothing. Nothing and no-one scared him. From drunken louts off steamers threatening to bash his brains in to the monstrous size spiders that inhabited our home, nothing swayed my father but now, here we were in this terrifying situation and my dad was too afraid to go and see off whatever was outside.

I did as I was told and stayed in bed trying to ignore the nightmare that was going on outside. I tried to rationalise the noise but I couldn't. There was no animal on this planet capable of making those sounds that I could hear so clearly through my tear stained pillow.

Then, quite suddenly, after nearly an hour, the noises stopped. They didn't fade away, they just stopped and all I could hear was the sound of my crying and the water as it dribbled through the small gap in the lock gates. I stayed where I was; still terrified in case the noises, or more importantly what was causing them came back but they didn't and as dawn approached I began to slip into an exhausted and restless sleep.

We did not hear the alarm that morning and once I did wake up I felt dazed and confused. Taking my cup of tea that daddy had made for me I walked outside to where the furor and mayhem the previous night had emanated from. I surveyed the scene bewildered. Where was the evidence? There should have been proof to the chaos that we all heard last night but there wasn't. Not a blade of grass was out of place. The flower beds were immaculate. There were no scratches on the paths and there should have been. I was expecting to see blood, fur and flesh scattered everywhere but there was nothing, nothing too prove that last night's events even took place. Feeling lost and defeated I went back inside.

Needless to say I was late for school that morning and as we drove out of Cookham my dad and I discussed the previous night. He had come to the same conclusion that I had, that there was nothing on this Earth that could have made those sounds. After all when they had finished had it of been an animal we would have heard it either run, swim or fly away.

"So, what do you think it was?" I asked.
My dad thought for a minute before answering. "If we are sure that there is nothing in the natural world that could have sounded like that then well lets just say that there are more things in Heaven and Earth than we are aware of and…" He never finished the sentence.

Many years later after we had left Cookham and moved to the Forest of Dean we visited my brother and his wife at their lock and although I do not know how or why, this episode became the point of conversation. My brother and his wife listened intently and then Shirley turned to David and said "Do you remember that night in Cookham when we were alone in the house?" At that point my brother turned visibly grey, made an excuse about having to do something outside and left. Intrigued by my brother's reaction I implored Shirley to recount her experience and this is what she told me.

It was shortly after as Shirley put it, they had started courting. Mum, dad and I had gone to visit someone. She couldn't remember who, but it was just her and David in the house. It was very late and they were in bed and asleep. Shirley remembers it well as it was not long after she had put curtains up at the window. It is odd thinking back but until Shirley came into our lives we never possessed a pair of curtains either upstairs or downstairs.

On the other side of the window there was a sloping roof which was directly above the lounge bay windows. Shirley said that something startled her awake although she is not sure what but when she rolled over she clearly saw the silhouetted figure of a person standing outside of the window. What frightened her most was that she knew that no-one could have been standing there due to the angle of the slope. Terrified she huddled back down under the covers and eventually fell fast asleep.

Much more recently I asked her to recount the story again for the purpose of this book and she was happy to do so. She said that her only regret was that she did not wake David who, when she told that following morning, refused to believe her. I asked her again what she thought it was and she still believes quite firmly that whatever it was, was not living and not of this world.

Chapter 9 – 1985

As years go this one for me could have been considered the calm before the storm. There was nothing amazing or particularly out of the ordinary that springs to mind about this year. I was studying for my O'Levels and even reading through my mother's diary it is very much concentrated on the weather and her getting ready to spend Christmas in Australia leaving me and my father home alone.

I do remember that during this year I was quite low, possibly even suffering with depression although I cannot remember why. I found school increasingly difficult to deal with and at one point I remember becoming quite disruptive and much later was told that many a concerned discussion was had about me in the staff room.

The highlight of my school year was playing the part of a slightly mad professor in a play called "Our Town."   It was an odd play to say the least but I must of played my part well as the applauds were the loudest and the longest for me even though I forget my lines and had to improvise on the spot. Other than my teacher I do not think anyone else noticed.

It is strange how a path in life can suddenly present itself and the decision that you make can determine the rest of your life and although I have had many paths presented to me this was to be the first. After the play a father of one of the children came up to me and asked if I would be interested in auditioning for a performance he was putting on in the West End. I do not know who he, or clearly remember what the play was but I do know I turned his offer down stating that I wanted to concentrate on my education. I often wonder where that could have led to but know that even if I did take up his offer; whatever it would have brought for me whether it be fame and wealth or the reverse side of that coin, I would not have been as happy as I am now.

Although my mother recorded a lot of the day-to-day happenings of our life she also noted down any major World events. Famous or infamous births, deaths, assignations, wars all got a mention and it was while reading through this year's diary that a selection of not so pleasant memories came back to me. Particularly throughout the 1970's and 1980's the World was plagued with tragedy after tragedy which although were all unrelated all had one thing in common. There were many deaths all caused by Airplane crashes. This year was no exception with a total of six major crashes spanning the year killing a total of one thousand, five hundred and eighty-eight people. It is my strong believe that when a large group of people die together their spiritual voices will almost join as one such must be the absolute terror and confusion to die in such a horrendous way.

The reason why I mention this is because I think I may have heard those that crashed and died while I slept. I particularly remember the crash that happened on the twenty-third of June of this year. It has been recorded as the sixth worst airplane disaster in history. A Boeing 747 exploded and crashed in the Atlantic Ocean just after seven o'clock on that Sunday morning. At this particular time I was sound asleep in my bed and supposedly knew nothing of this. The thing is I remember my dream as I remember many others as if I had dreamt them last night. All I could see in my dream was a huge expanse of blood coloured water and what appeared to be bodies floating on the surface. I remember waking and almost knowing the news before my father told me.

Dreams foretelling air disasters were not the only bad dreams that I suffered although strangely enough since the birth of my eldest daughter in 1994 I have not had one since.

There is however, one dream that is worth mentioning although if I am honest I am not sure which year it occurred in. It could have been this year or the year either side.

My father had two young men working for him who both drove black minis. They were lovely lads, one who I thought more of as a brother and the other well, let us just say that the nickname I gave him was 'Sex God!' One afternoon the brotherly one asked me if he could borrow some money as he was going to see his girlfriend straight from work. I cannot remember how much or indeed exactly what it was for but as he promised to pay it back the following day, I agreed.

That night I had the most terrible nightmare. I dreamt I saw his car smashed up and covered in blood. I laid awake for most of the night praying that just before nine he would drive in and all would be well. Imagine my relief when he did exactly that? By the way I greeted him I think he realized that I was acting a little odd and later in the morning when he paid his debt he enquired to my over exuberant welcome. I explained my dream to him and told him how relieved I was when I saw him drive up, both he and his mini intact. To say that he went rather pale was putting it mildly and I remember saying "But you are ok?"

He explained to me that he did not take his mini to see his girlfriend as planned but went home and for reasons that I cannot remember, took his mother's car instead. His mother's car was red in colour and yes, he did have an accident although not a serious one. I remember yelling at him to be more careful in the future.

Throughout my life I have had two reoccurring nightmares that still plague me to this day. They are usually brought on by extreme stress and although on paper they seem quite tame, in the blackness on night when I wake up screaming they are terrifying and leave me feeling cold and sick with fear. The first one is set in the very distant past and depict my mother and myself as a young girl walking along the edge of the main island upstream to collect milk. We are both dressed as old fashioned milk maids and are even carrying the buckets on yokes over our shoulders. This in itself is not frightening but it is what we are walking past that my mother cannot see that terrifies me so much. The lines of trees that we are walking past are all dead and diseased. Most are just hollow trunks of various sizes. As we walk past them out of each trunk lurches a tree ogre reaching out to grab me. They too vary in shape and size and are all hideously ugly with green, diseased mossy skin, parts of their faces hanging off and huge bulging eyes that slide in and out of their sockets. In all the years I have had the dream I have never reached the end of the journey.

My second nightmare is by far the worst and even just thinking about it gives me a feeling of dread and foreboding. I am in a large house, almost a stately home and I am playing hide and seek with my friends who I never actually see. I am the seeker of the game and I have found myself in the attic. The attic is huge with dark, dusty, ominous corners and shadows but it is not this that scares me. As I am about to leave the attic I hear a noise. It is the sound of fingernails tapping on glass. I turn and see a small window so high up that I can see the chimney tops through it. As I realise where the sound is coming from I start to scream and it is my screams that wake me for on the other side of this small window is a small, fully clothed monkey.

I have never known the origins of this dream until I began researching this book. I was looking through a pile of old photographs and I came across this one of me taken in 1972. When I saw what I was holding I dropped the photo in shock. Even now I still find it very unnerving that a photograph that I have no recollection of being taken could have imprinted the memory so deep into my subconscious. I suppose it is another example of the 'Circle of Life.'

Taken on South Parade Pier, South Sea, in 1970

Chapter 10 – 1986

This year began I suppose as every year begins when you live in the UK; cold, bleak and miserable. It was made worse by my mother's absence. She was now sunning herself in Ausi and would be for the next two months while we were left at home to fend for ourselves. Fending, if you will excuse the nautical term, was about right. Again, I cannot remember Christmas but the concerns that I had voiced to my school regarding my mother's holiday were not unfounded. I discovered that my father could function without my mum but that was all. He could get me to school and back again and he could do his job but that was about it. He could not cope with time on his own and nothing to occupy it. Most mornings I would come downstairs to empty bottles of alcohol, ashtrays overfilling with cigarette ends and the air saturated with the smell of stale smoke. I saw him drunk on many occasions but he had the remarkable ability to sober up to take and pick me up from my baby-sitting job.

In many respects this job saved my life. For one it got me out of the house. Not just from my father you understand, because I loved him dearly but from the house itself. At home I felt like my ticket had expired and I was waiting to be evicted such was the atmosphere in my rooms. It is only with hindsight that I can realise that the warnings were there; it was just a shame and circumstance that I was too young and naive to realise them.

My mother was not due home until the first of March and so for two months we blundered on, my father and I. My mother's diary tells of telephone calls from me where I expressed my concerns but knowing me I probably put the proverbial face on it and she did not realise the seriousness of the matter. But of course, she did not know what else was going on.

It was to be my final year at school and revision for my O'Levels were taking centre stage. As I have stated previously I was not the most academic of children and so the few that I took I wanted to do well in. This unfortunately did not include mathematics. It was not then and still is not now my strong subject. In truth, given half a chance you would not catch me near it but now with two children it is a subject that I have to at least try and understand. If I am honest however, my husband deals with this kind of homework. Back in this year however it was different and it was not until later on in the year that I sought the help of one of our summer assistants for their expertise on the subject. Until then, I was effectively, on my own.

Baby-sitting took up most of my evenings and so although I knew that this episode happened in the early part of this year, I am not entirely sure when. Memory tells me that it was the February but with my mother abroad I cannot confirm this. What I do know is that I was alone at the time so I can only assume that my father was either visiting my brother, running an errand for his employers (which, was not unusual) or shopping at the warehouse that was open late in Reading where he had an account.

As I had stated earlier the upstairs area of our house especially my two bedrooms were giving me serious cause for concern. I cannot describe it specifically but it was as if the air was being sucked out of them. There was a feeling of almost deadness to them as if I should not have been there, I certainly didn't feel welcome anymore but had no choice each night but to sleep there. After my mother's return she states in her diary how upset I became when I could not do my revision downstairs because my father was watching something on television. The reason I would not work upstairs was because, quite simply I was too scared.

The circumstances surrounding this particular episode I remember as clearly as if it happened five minutes ago. I remember everything (except precisely where my father was) what homework I had, what I watched on television before I started my homework, even that I had to put logs on the fire so that it did not go out.

My homework consisted of English Literature and mathematics. The math I do not remember precisely except that I struggled with them and that it involved algebra, an area I was particularly weak on. I do recall that it was the subject that I started with as I wanted to get it out of my way and I know that I spent at least an hour on it before giving up and feeling close to tears. I remember I made myself a cup of tea before embarking on the English and it was whilst I was drinking my tea that I realised that I had left my poetry book upstairs in my bedroom.

My English Literature O'Level was the one subject that I had to work extra hard on not because I wasn't any good at it because I was. It was because I had chosen not to do all of it. Two years previously when we had been given our subjects for our exams I could not have been more pleased to learn the areas that we were covering in our literature exam. 'As You Like It' was to be our Shakespeare play, poems on war or people (I chose war) were to be our poetry section and the classic novel was to be 'War of the Worlds.' I could not have been happier as I loved not only the book but also the music and many of the films that had been produced as a result of this great classic. So can you imagine my disappointment when instead of 'War of the Worlds' we were handed 'Silas Marner?' Now I am told that this is a wonderful piece of literary work but in honesty, I was not impressed. Like all books that I read I gave it a first page chance but needless to say it did not fill me with inspiration or even indeed the urge to read on and so after struggling through the page I calmly put the book on my desk and told my teacher that I was not reading any more of it! She replied by telling my quite matter-of-fact that I would not pass my exam without reading it. Looking at her straight in the eye I replied "You just watch me!"

But tonight my homework was not on Silas Marner but to choose two poems from two different wars and comment on how they are still relevant today. I was actually looking forward to doing it until I realised that I had left my poetry book upstairs. I was not thinking about the atmosphere or whatever else you want to call it that was in my room but it was more to do with the fact that upstairs it was, to be honest bloody cold. In our lounge where I was working there was a roaring fire filling downstairs with heat but once I was through the lounge door, well it was a bit like stepping into Narnia without the fur coats! Knowing that I had no choice I opened the door and headed for the stairs.

As soon as I rounded the corner and stood at the foot of our stairs I knew something was wrong. I had the same feeling I get now when I know that there is a spider lurking somewhere in the vicinity. It was a feeling of being watched. It was also the feeling of impending doom. Have you ever stood on what should be a really busy street but there be nobody else around? There are no people, no traffic, no dogs barking; no sound at all? You stand there wondering if civilization has come to an end and you are the only living thing left. Then just as you wonder whether you should start panicking a lorry comes hurtling past you and the moment is gone and normality is resumed. Well that is as close to how I can describe how I felt at that moment but also combined with the feeling that I had to go up those stairs.

There was also an overwhelming sense of presence and it was not a good feeling. Almost in tears I took a deep breath and ran up the steps to my room. Unbelievably my room felt fine. I saw my book lying on my bed where I had left it and all seemed calm and well, normal in fact. Beginning to think that I was going mad I chastised myself and switching the light off after me, went back onto the landing to go downstairs.

I do not know how long this next episode lasted, for it seemed to go on for eternity. When I recall the incident, in my mind it is played in slow motion, every second dragged out in terrifying elongated detail. I cannot recall the incident in real time but I suppose thinking about it all these years later it actual time was no more than a minute.

I was standing at the top of the stairs about to go down. I had placed my right hand on the banister rail to steady myself and in my left hand I held my book. My right leg swung out so that my right foot would descend to the next step when suddenly I stopped breathing. My leg was still suspended, hovering above the step but the fear that had entered me was overwhelming. The real terror was that I could see my fear. As I had gone to descend the stairs a hand, had with force, slammed from behind me onto my left shoulder. I stood there absolutely rigid, unable to scream knowing that there was no living soul in the house but me. With almost physical pain I slowly glanced down to look at my left shoulder and there lying on it I could see long, pale fingers the colour of milk. The nails albeit the same colour as the skin, were beautifully manicured and I knew at once that the hand belonged (surprisingly) to a female. I then had a vision as if I was standing behind myself. I could see the back of me standing at the top of the stairs and I could see the hand resting on my shoulder. I could also see that the hand was attached to a wrist and the wrist to an arm that went up to just below an elbow. But there was no elbow. In fact after the lower part of the arm there was nothing else.

It was this vision that brought me out of my trance-like state and my fight or flight instinct that we all have took over. My brain chose flight and I literally hurled myself down those stairs. There was no walking calmly, no running, I landed at the bottom of the stairs and half staggered half crawled into our lounge. Amazingly I still had the book in my hand and I threw it onto the sofa, accidently hitting the cat with it as it landed.

Shaking with fear I went straight for my father's bottle of whiskey that was in our cabinet and shakily poured myself a huge glassful. I cannot remember ever being as terrified as I was then and I am sad to say that it was the only time in my school life that I ever handed in homework late.

Thankfully on the first of March my mother arrived home and I knew that our life would return to some form of normality. My father's drinking would return to its typical amounts and I would have someone to talk to that would not spend the majority of the time nagging me.

The incident with the floating, ghostly arm troubled me not just back then but to this day. At first I was just petrified, the experience played on my mind and I hated having to go upstairs and go to sleep. I decided the best way to cope with the situation was to avoid it as much as possible and so homework was then completed downstairs and I spent as little time as possible in the house. Looking much older than my fifteen years meant that when I was not working I could join my friends in our local pub and never once be questioned about my age. I found that going to the pub was beneficial in more than one way. Not only did it keep me away from home but the alcohol that I drunk meant that when I did get home I would go to sleep much quicker.

It was not long after my mother's return that it soon felt like she had never been away and with spring just around the corner, the days became longer and life became more enjoyable. Upstairs it had gone quiet. Nothing moved or switched on or off unless I moved or switched it on or off and I fell into the false sense of security believing that whatever it was had gone.

All remained calm during spring and early summer in our household. Although the weather was mixed the river traffic was steady and my parents were both busy attending to their various needs. The evening steamer trips meant additional work not only letting them through but providing them with food in the form of fish and chip meals and with the shop busy neither of my parents would be in bed before midnight.

Then in June came a phone call to say that my eldest cousin was ill in hospital and it was not good. My mother's presence was needed and within a couple of weeks she had flown out to be at her sister's side. Reading through her diary it tells of the uncertainty of the condition of my cousin but he was drastically ill. Tests eventually revealed that he had a condition called Cardiomyopathy and that he needed a heart transplant. By this time my mother had returned home. In those days heart transplants were still in their infancy and my aunt had to go on television to advertise their plight. Thankfully a donor was found and his transplant took place. Although the doctors warned that the new heart would only last ten years I am pleased to say that he remains healthy and is happily married with children.

In mid-July I took over as my father's summer assistant thankful to have something to fill my days. I loved working on the lock and although the weather continued to be a mixture of sunshine and showers it never affected how I dressed. Boaters were amazed that I never wore shoes and could run up and down the lock-side attending to the boats and never once hurt my feet. However, I did have a pair of trainers that I kept in the lock office. These only saw my feet when the river inspectors came into sight; health and safety meant that I must wear 'the correct footwear apparel' they told me but as soon as they were gone, so were my shoes!

The end of August brought my exam results and I was pleased that what revision I had done had paid off. I passed all that I took even the English Literature exam of which when it came to questions on 'Silas Marner' I knew nothing about. It would be worth going back to school to collect my certificates just to say "I told you so," to my teacher!

September came and so with it came college. I was greatly excited about becoming a college student but it was not long before I realized that it was not school that I did not like but the education system in general. It seemed to matter not how nice a person you were or how much common sense you had but what clothes you wore and how you looked. The more I went the more I realized that it was not for me.

September rolled into October and although I had been at college I had still been working weekends for my father. It had been a summer of few incidents and now as I finished my last weekend on the lock the realization came that with my sixteenth birthday rapidly approaching my childhood was all but at an end and my future was now down to me. However, although I still believe this sometimes things are thrown at you and are out of your control. Just three days before my birthday I spent an excruciating night in bed where no one heard my cries for help. My stomach felt as if it was being ripped open and by the early hours I had managed to climb out of bed in order to get help. I only made it as far as my door but as it was closed I could go no further as I did not have the strength to open it. I collapsed on the floor and spent the rest of the night banging my head against the wall in an attempt to psychologically stop or move the pain. By morning I was still in agony and after a visit to the doctors I found myself in hospital undergoing an operation for an emergency appendectomy. My birthday celebrations were put on hold and replaced by the nurses standing around by bed singing 'happy birthday to you' on the great day at some ungodly hour of the morning.

Things went from bad to worse as I then developed an infection and could not go home until two days later. After being put on antibiotics I was told the infection would sort itself out but was not told how. I found out how a week or so later when green muck started leaking out in huge volumes from my new scar. I woke up to find my bed soaking and covered in the sticky liquid. A trip to the doctors resolved the situation with the help of a knitting needle type instrument that was inserted into the end of my scar and over a pint of fluid was drained out of me.

The remainder of the year came and went and I welcomed in the New Year with a new feeling of expectancy little realizing how 1987 would change the way we lived forever.

Chapter 11 – 1987

Death, in whatever vehicle it chooses to arrive, actually has only five ways that it can take you to that ultimate destination. These modes of transport, however uncomfortable, are accidental death, suicide, murder, sickness and old age or natural causes that leads to death. In whichever vehicle that you end up traveling there are only two speeds, very quickly, such as my brother's death where we were told he died instantly or, as in the case of my Gran, slowly and often with great pain. In my eyes the death of Cookham Lock took the latter speed. As cancer begins to eat at the flesh and often goes unnoticed so the cancer began to seep this year into our very existence.

The year began calmly enough. Our main concern was our dog. Although he had been diagnosed with Hip Dysplasia, huge patches of fur were beginning to disappear from areas over his back. A visit to the vets came with the information that he now had eczema. More lotions and potions were prescribed for him. His appearance was obviously so bad that, unbeknown to us, we were reported to the RSPCA. In early February an inspector from the charity turned up with concerns that we were mistreating our dog. After talking with us, seeing the vet's bill and then witnessing the dog walking along the side of our garden hedge scratching his back and side leaving behind bits of dead skin and hair on the spiky twigs, he went away satisfied.

Although worried about our dog I had other things on my mind. It had been a year since the terrifying encounter in the upstairs of our home had sent me almost running for my life and until recently I had put the incident to the back of my mind. Now, every day when I came home from college my bedroom seemed somehow different. It was difficult to determine exactly what had changed as my room never looked the tidiest. On a weekend in early March I tidied my room, much to my parent's surprise. Pleased with my efforts I thought I would now be able to notice exactly what was being altered. When I arrived home from college the following Monday it was not difficult to see the changes.

The mixture of emotions that I had when I opened the door of my bedroom left me feeling sick and confused. The terror of knowing that it had happened again and knowing that it was still going on even in my absence was overwhelming. But I was also angry, bloody angry in fact. My room looked worse than before the weekend. All the bedding was on the floor, some of the clothes that had been left on the table were now strewn around and all the posters that had been firmly attached to the walls were now lying in amongst the bedding. I sat on my bed and cried. I did not understand what was going on. Were these spirits just trying to annoy me or were they trying to get my attention and tell me something?   I did not and still do not know but I often wonder if they knew what was to come and were trying to warn me.

Other areas of my life were also not going to plan. College was turning into a nightmare. I had been accepted onto a course to study the NNEB certificate and part of this meant going into a local primary school to work alongside the teachers. The written side of the course was fine and in my opinion all that was needed was a modicum of common sense. However, the teacher who was at my placement had other ideas about what career path I should be taking. I had taken an instant dislike to this woman not only personally but professionally as well. I did not like the rough almost violent way she treated the children. It all started going down- hill when I had voiced my concerns after witnessing her manhandle a child into her coat who obviously did not want to wear it. She was so forceful with this child that I am sure she must have left bruises but when she slapped the child I decided that enough was enough. The decision to leave was an easy one particularly as I received no support from the college. A few weeks after I had left I received a telephone call from the college to say that the woman was no longer at the school as she had been caught hitting one of her charges and so, would I like to come back?   I declined. I now had a job in an off license in our local town and was working most evenings babysitting. I didn't have time for education; I was now too busy earning money.

The last Sunday in March brought with it an eerie surprise. Unbeknown to me we were to have a new member of the household. Friends of my parents who kept a boat at our lock owned a Siamese cat. When not boating they resided in London where they had been recently adopted by another less than pedigree kitten. The problem was that their Siamese took an instant almost hateful dislike to this kitten. Rather than take it to an animal shelter they asked my father if we would like it. Much to my mother's amazement my father agreed. When I came home from my day job there was this kitten sitting on the window ledge waiting for me. The surprise should have been a pleasant one but when I saw the kitten for the first time my reaction somewhat shocked my mother who was in the room with me. Upon seeing the kitten I screamed and became hysterical. Could no-one see what I could see?   Were the spirits that abided in our home playing a cruel trick on me?   On first sight the kitten (who was approximately twelve weeks old) looked exactly like Spud, our old cat. It took several minutes for my mother to calm me down so that she could explain the arrival of this not so spectral feline.

I named her Spudy and her and I became great friends. She would follow me everywhere while I was at home and it was never really a problem until one late afternoon when I was off to the pub.

I suppose it is at this point that I should mention my local drinking establishment. I had been frequenting the Ferry Inn for some time, far longer in fact than I should have been!   The pub sat just upstream of the lock area on the main river bank and was heavily used by boaters and land lubbers alike!   In the evenings it was a popular location and often heaving with people of all ages. Although I did not look it I was probably the youngest drinker in there and because of my attachment to the lock I was well known and well liked. My eldest brother had drunk in there in his younger days and his funeral wake had been held there. On evenings when it was too busy to get to the bar I would put three songs on the juke box so that the bar staff would know I was waiting. 'Get it on' by 'T-Rex,' 'A Horse with No Name' by 'America' and 'Free's' 'All right Now' became my songs. So much so that sometimes when it wasn't busy the landlord would put them on for me anyway.

Spudy had been to the pub on many occasions with me and it had never been a problem before. The customers quite enjoyed seeing a cat sitting on the table as it made a difference from there being just dogs in the beer garden. However, on one occasion the cat did not make it as far as the pub. We were walking across the common when she was spotted by a spaniel who immediately gave chase. My cat ran for her life across the common and headed for a small brook. Without even realizing it was there she found herself in the water and with a speed that defied belief she almost threw herself out of the brook and then flew up a tree so fast she was like a blur. All the coaxing in the world would not bring her down and so I had to resort to going back home and asking my dad for help. He came out and to my amazement climbed twenty or so feet up into the tree and brought her back down with him. Although he heard my "thank you," it was somewhat drowned out with his comment of "Bloody animals!"

However traumatized my cat was after this event I do not know as it certainly never stopped her going to the pub with me. Before we reached the common she would always jump up onto and then travel on my shoulder so as to be out of reach of her canine foes!

During April I started working for my father again as summer assistant. The climate was favourable making the job even more enjoyable but as the days slid into May there was an air of change that had nothing to do with the weather. In early May we received the sad news that Stan Pope the local farmer had died suddenly. Then, I through my own silly fault, whilst at a pub, put my arm accidently through a glass pane in a door and sliced it open resulting in twenty or so stitches. Also, our beloved dog seemed to be getting more poorly.

But there was something else. At some point earlier it had been agreed by the powers that be that Odney weir, our only drivable access to and from the mainland was no longer safe. If we needed a fire engine there was serious doubt that the weir would hold the weight and it had been agreed that work would start in May to build a new weir just down from the old one. On the eighteenth of May huge vehicles carrying all the equipment began arriving, causing chaos in the vicinity and rapidly turning the beautiful green area surrounding the weir into a building site. Terrapin buildings and portable toilets were set up and as various people began to inspect the sight so the weir gates began to be left open allowing walkers onto the island. Although none of us voiced our concerns about what lay ahead for the future my mother's thoughts that she wrote on the nineteenth of May describe it eloquently. *"I feel so bitter about this place now. Although it may pass I doubt it will."*

Odney Weir before it was demolished. The new weir was built only a few feet below this one. (Copyright © Ian Pethers)

My father had many faults but one was by far the greatest and the most annoying – he was always right. Whether the subject was politics, economics, history, astro-physics it made no difference, he could never be proved wrong! There was only one occasion that I can recall where this aggravating irk proved to be hilariously funny. He had been in consultation with the engineers that were to rebuild the weir and after listening to their plans he had told them that their ideas would not work. Their initial plan was to float a massive crane on a barge out into the middle of the weir stream just below the weir itself. They were then going to tie it off at either end so that they could use it to move the larger pieces of the structure with ease. Very strongly my father told them that their plan would fail but they were insistent that it would work as they had used this process many times before. Shaking his head my father walked away from them warning them that the next meeting that they would have would begin with him telling them "I told you so."

Ignoring his warning the said plan was put into action. The crane was maneuvered onto the barge and floated out into the weir stream where it was tied off. This obviously took some time and so as it was near the end of the day when it was completed the engineers and workmen called time and went home. Imagine their horror and surprise at the sight that greeted them when they arrived the following morning. Embarrassed and bemused they walked down to the lock to consult with my father. He walked back up to the weir with them and at a distance I followed curious to see what had gone wrong. The sight that met our eyes verged on the ridiculous and resembled an old Ealing comedy. All around the weir highly educated men stood and scratched their heads unable to ascertain what had gone wrong. My father and I must have spotted the situation at the same time as we both burst out laughing and I heard my father splutter the words he had promised to say.

The barge in the centre of the weir stream had vanished, sunk with the weight of the crane beneath the torrent of water that flowed from the weir. The crane itself had slipped to an odd angle and was now only visible from the neck up. It resembled a dinosaur reaching out of the water. "It's the bloody Loch Ness monster," I laughed with tears streaming down my face.

As if speaking to a child my father patiently explained what had gone wrong.
"We do not understand," the qualified engineers said. "We have executed this procedure many times before and this has never happened."
"From my understanding you have only ever done this on a canal?" my father enquired failing to keep the annoyance out of his voice.
"Yes," confirmed the qualified engineers. "So?"
My father's patience evaporated. "Rivers flow and have a current. Canals are man-made and they have no current. The water has flowed off the weir and straight into the barge sinking the bloody thing."   With that and still laughing we turned and walked back to the lock leaving them to sort out their mess.

The work on the weir continued and would do so for many months to come and with it brought more problems than we could ever imagine. Because the weir gates were left unlocked walkers would continue to come in and wander around the island. Often when they came to leave they found they could not as it had gone closing time and the gates had then been firmly locked. Although the next two incidences I believe are firmly linked together the resulting third incident may not have been perpetrated by the same people but the police believed that either they were responsible or it was the work of the IRA.

On the twenty-fourth of May a group of people consisting of husband, wife, two children and grandparents found their way onto the island and subsequently found themselves locked in. That evening as we were sitting down to dinner there came a knock at the door and the group stood there complaining that they could not get off the island. It had become a daily chore to go up to the weir and let people out. The frustration was enormous as the weir gates held a huge notice that clearly said 'NO UNAUTHORISED ACCESS' in massive letters. Time and time again it was ignored and this particular evening we all had had enough.

"We can't get off the island," they moaned as I opened the door to the group.

"Your choices are stay until nine in the morning, see if you can get a boat to give you a lift or climb around the gates," I told them and shut the door on them and went to finish my dinner. Ten minutes later they knocked on the door again and demanded that I let them out. Grabbing the keys and calling the dog I once again left my dinner to go cold and walked the distance up to the weir to let them out. "Did you not see the notice," I asked them? They refused to answer. Walking just ahead of them as we approached the weir I asked the two children if they would be returning to school after their holidays and they confirmed that they would be. In a voice loud enough for their parents to hear I suggested that when they went back to school they took their parents with them so they could teach their mum and dad to read. As I unlocked the gate and let them out I drew their attention to the notice and pointed out that it was in plain sight and in plain English. Then locking the gate firmly behind me I returned home. But it was not, I believe the last I was to hear from them.

Three days later I walked into town to collect our mail from the local garage. There were several letters for us and one of them caught my attention. I cannot remember how it was addressed but it seemed to be for me and upon reading the first line I knew I was right. It was what is commonly called a poison pen letter and the phrase the pen is mightier than the sword was never so more felt by me than then. I can only remember that first line but that was more than enough. "To the fat bitch with the big dog…" I was incensed and very upset. Why were people so bloody selfish? No one in their right mind would enter a stranger's garden and wander round without permission yet they thought they had the right to do it here? Little did we realize that this was just to be the start of a much more serious incident?

It rained heavily during the night prior to the thirty-first leaving the early morning heavy, damp and humid but by mid-morning the sun came out daring it to be a beautiful day. Sunshine always brought the boaters out and the effect on the last day of May proved to be no exception. By mid-morning the river was heaving with boats large and small and it was difficult to see the waters for the amount of traffic that seemed to want to descend on our small part of the Thames.

It was either late morning or early afternoon when the lock telephone rang and after answering it dad announced that he had to go up to Cookham Weir to do some work. I waved him off more than happy and more than able to cope with the quantity of boats that were appearing. Cookham Weir was a good fifteen minutes' walk away and with the work that he had to do I did not expect to see him for the best part of an hour.

I had completed only about two lock-full's of boats and was at the bottom of the lock letting out the water when I saw my dad approach the lock. I was busy chatting to some boat owners that we knew when his voice interrupted our conversation.
"Rachel! Office! Now," he bellowed! The only time I had ever heard him use that tone of voice was when I was in trouble and so

somewhat perplexed I excused myself from the chat and followed him into the office. I was sure I hadn't done anything wrong and was desperately trying to think why he had shouted at me in that way. As I entered the office I heard the tail end of a phone call that went something along the lines of "…As soon as I have informed my summer assistant of the situation I will be there."   He put the phone down, picked up the pedestal chains and key and handed them to me. His words are as clear as me today as they were then.

"There is a bomb on the weir. Let these boats out and then shut down the lock. Nothing moves. Just tell people that there is a problem with the water. For the love of God do not panic them. I have informed the police and they will be here shortly. Bomb squad will not be far behind. This is not fair on you but you will have to cope alone. I have to go up and let them all in and then show them where the bomb is, OK?"

Knowing that my father was about to put his life on the line for the safety of all that he loved I had no choice but to carry out his wishes and seeing at least twenty boats moored up beneath lock I knew that my news to them was not going to go down well. It was the era of the IRA and the thought that they had finally found the Achilles heel of this part of the country scared the hell out of me. I knew that if the bomb went off it would be devastating; we could say goodbye to all the houses in the vicinity below us and that several locks down would not be able to cope with the onslaught of water that would be coming their way. It would be like an inland Tsunami.

Picking up the loud speaker in the other hand that we kept in the cupboard below the telephone I left the office and went to the bottom of the lock where the water had now left the lock and the gates were ready to open. Merrily I waved goodbye to the boaters as they left the lock but as soon as the last boat had exited much to the surprise of those waiting to enter, I shut the gates and waved my arms in front of me indicating that they could not come in. Then I locked up the hydraulic pedestal and put the chain around the manual wheel operation locking that firmly as well. Only when I was sure that no one could use it did I pick up the loud hailer and walk as far as I could to the bottom of the lock. Lifting the loud-hailer to my lips, in a clear voice I began:

"Ladies and gentleman, your attention please," I made sure it sounded like a statement and not a question. "A problem with the water has been reported and it is necessary for you to remain where you are. I apologise for the disruption but it is necessary. I have been informed that you are all perfectly safe but I cannot let you through. Please, those of you that can hear me can you please pass this message back to the boats that are behind you. As soon as I have more information I will let you know. Thank you for your co-operation." I then moved away from the bottom of the lock, walked to the top of the lock, locked the pedestal and repeated myself. Then I walked back and after shutting the door behind me, replaced the loud hailer in the office and made two telephone calls to the locks above and below us informing them of the situation.

Exiting the office I became completely surrounded by angry and confused boaters all demanding an explanation and all demanding that I let them through the lock immediately. Nearly repeating myself I again explained what I could and told them that as it was such a lovely day they should at least be thankful for that. Still not happy they drifted back to their boats. All it is except one gentleman who was not going to let me get away with it without having his rather rude say.

"Girl," he began and oh how I remember him emphasizing that word, "Just who the hell do you think you are telling me I cannot go through this lock?
"I am the summer assistant, I am also the Lock Keeper's daughter, I have told you all I can and my only suggestion is you do as I have asked."
"I am not standing for this," he bellowed directly into my face, his nose almost touching mine.
"Not standing for what," came a calm, measured voice from behind him? One of the more senior members of the Thames Valley Police stood there smiling oh, so pleasantly.
"This girl is refusing to let us through the lock. It is preposterous."
"As far as you are concerned whatever this young *woman* tells you, you take as law. Either that or I will have you arrested, your choice?"

Strangely enough the man skulked away and it was the last I saw of him other than to let him through the lock many hours later.

The policeman in question was in charge of our section of the River Police and after a general conversation he directed me towards another, this time police lady who I knew who asked me about the letter I received. To this day I am not sure who planted the bomb. I find it hard to believe that the family that I let out under less than pleasant tones would have sunk so far as to cause that much disruption. But to my knowledge I have never heard of the IRA planting a hoax bomb. Because that is what it turned out to be, nothing more than an elaborate, well made hoax. Consequently we finished late that day as boats were backed up well beyond what we could see but with the exception of the one rather rude gentleman everyone was extremely patient and needless to say my mother made a huge profit in the shop. She had the ultimate captured audience.

Although the incident with the bomb was over and done with I had been asked to be extra vigilant with those that came wandering onto our island. I was left with a feeling of distrust and a growing dislike of a place that I had loved and known intimately all my life. Strangers on the island seemed common place and on one occasion at a barbeque with some friends I may have overacted when I learnt that one of them supported the IRA. In a fit of rage I physically dragged this person off the island and refused to let her come back in.

A couple of days later my feelings were shattered again when our beloved St Bernard had to go to the vets and did not return. The eczema on his back had turned cancerous and large globules of black, diseased blood dripped out of him from the raw patches on his back. It was a horrid end for a beautiful animal.

It was still early June and another small piece of information came by way of my brother. The information in itself to most would seem unimportant but it proved to be the start of a trend that remains today. My brother reported that he was six hundred boats down on last year in June alone and it was still only the fifth of the month. I laugh now when I hear through the watery grape vine how busy the 'new' Lock-Keepers are. When I speak to those that have been on the river all their life and are soon due for retirement they tell me what we knew back then. The river was dying.

June was not an easy month for any of us. Not only did we have to contend with the turmoil of the weir rebuilding but also the lock was not working properly. This meant that we had to work the lock the old fashioned way by hand. Instead of flicking a switch to open or close the gates and sluices we had to wind a wheel which added nearly half an hour to each lock-full that we processed. No-one seemed to know what was wrong with the lock and often dad and I were out working until gone eleven at night. Considering we were supposed to finish at seven they were not bad hours that we were putting in for absolutely no reward or thanks.

It was in the middle of June that we received a 'present' from our employers! This year had brought with it, along with everything else, a massive environmental problem. We had run out of space to burn our rubbish. There are only so many holes you can dig to get rid of your waste and the part of the island where we dug the holes had now been filled. Although this situation was no good for us it was very good for the rat population which had grown massively. Earlier on in the year my mother had all but dragged one of the river inspectors to our land fill to show them the problem. Now, they had answered our situation by providing us with an incinerator. It was like winning the lottery!

The summer rolled on and it seemed that our standard of living was deteriorating like the weather. The mess at the weir caused by the rebuilding was intolerable and now as the lock was still not working properly more engineers had turned up to dig long, deep trenches through our garden to put down new cables. It seemed whichever way we turned we were living in a building site. The situation caused nothing but arguments between my parents. My father seemed almost apathetic towards it and when my mother spoke out and voiced her opinion to those in charge it just seemed to make matters worse. By the middle of August the situation was getting to me as well. The workmen had been given permission to mix cement right outside our kitchen window – it seemed that no matter how big the island was we just could not get away from the mess and disruption. The lock still refused to work and the sight of workmen, surveyors and engineers standing around scratching their head and getting in my way became too much. At one point I stormed off of the lock telling one of them that as he could not do his job maybe he could do mine!

With our World slowly being turned upside-down I had been giving more and more thought to my future career. My parents had decided to emigrate to Australia once my dad retired and at first I did not want to go with them. Watching my world being destroyed around me I had changed my mind and applied to the Perth Police Force. I was turned down. I then had the idea to join the Royal Navy but that idea was disregarded when I learnt that women could not work on board ships. What was the point of joining the Navy if I couldn't go to sea?   I was at a loss. The obvious answer was to continue on the river and hopefully become a Lock Keeper myself but out of all the careers I could choose this was the one that my father refused. He made it perfectly clear that while he was around no way would I become a Lock keeper.

By September things were no better and the problems that all the building work was causing intensified. There was an accident on the lock, not a serious one but nevertheless one that required an ambulance. The ambulance was duly called but when the paramedics arrived they found that they could not get over the weir and so they had to leave the vehicle and walk down. Had the accident been of a serious nature I dread to think what the repercussions could have been?

Early October saw me having to go into hospital for a small operation. Earlier on in the year I had a dentist appointment which did not go according to plan. I had to have all of my wisdom teeth out as they were impacting and causing me great pain. My usual dentist was on holiday during this time but informed me that he would leave me in the excellent hands of a private dentist who would be covering for him. To say that I have never been a fan of the dentist is putting it mildly and I was more than a little nervous at the thought of having four teeth out. It did not go well from the start.

The dentist struggled to get my teeth out, broke an instrument in the process and at that point I became hysterical. The situation was not improved when the dentist slapped me around the face causing me with blood running from my mouth, to leap up from the chair and run screaming from the surgery!   As a result of this episode it was decided that I would have the teeth removed under anaesthetic in hospital! Thankfully this time all went according to plan and I was released a couple of days later.

Approximately two weeks later I had to return to the hospital for a check-up. The out patients area for the dentists was situated at the rear of the hospital in a small, run-down terrapin building. To reach this building I had to go past the rear entrance of the chapel of rest. As I approached, the rear chapel double doors opened and two men exited, pushing a trolley which although covered in a white sheet, obviously held a dead body. Parked outside of the chapel was an ambulance which I presume was there to transport the body to a Funeral Parlour. As the men wheeled the body to the vehicle neither noticed the curb and consequently one of the men tripped and landed on his bottom. Unfortunately, at the same time one of the trolley's wheels went over the curb and the movement caused the cadaver to move. A lifeless arm flopped out from under the sheet rapidly followed by the torso. Never in my life have I seen two men move so quickly to cover up a naked female!   Both of the men apologized to me but I must admit that with my rather sick sense of humour I found the whole incident incredibly funny and could not help but giggle all the way through my appointment!

I believe the night of the fifteenth of October will stay in the minds of many forever. I am sure that most people when asked 'Where were you when the great storm hit' could immediately conjure a reply and I was no different. That night I was baby-sitting and had taken a friend with me. The people that I baby-sat for worked in a hotel and were often not home until two or three in the morning and this night was no exception. The weather man had said that the winds would not be that strong but as the evening drew on we knew he had made a mistake. I sat in the house with my friend with my young charge sound asleep in her bed and began to wonder how that night was going to end. We had lost the electricity fairly early on in the evening and had scrabbled around looking for candles. Even in the safety of this house we could barely hear ourselves speak and had to resort to almost shouting at one another just to be heard above the roar of the wind outside. At around one in the morning the lady returned home concerned that we could not get home safely. She had organized a taxi for us and gave the driver very strict instructions that he was to drop us off at my home. I explained to him about the weir but told him it was safe to cross. He agreed on the door to door delivery. However, upon arriving at the weir he went back on his word and refused to take us over saying that he would be blown into the river if he tried to drive across. For many minutes I begged him to drive us across stating that a car was heavier than we were and it would not be safe for us to try and cross but he didn't care. He almost dragged us out of the car more intent now on getting him safely home.

Stepping out of the car was like stepping into Hell without the heat. Immediately both my friend and I were nearly dragged off our feet and trying to speak to each other was impossible. We clung onto the weir gates and I bellowed what I thought was to be the safest route. All around us we could hear the sounds of breaking wood, crashing metal and above all of that the wind. The wind so loud it was terrifying; not even thunder could match this volume and its force was even more formidable. We had to physically throw ourselves from piece of machinery to piece of machinery just to hold on and not be blown over into the treacherous waters below. Once off the weir matters did not improve. We clung to each other as we struggled back to the house, buffeted by the gusts and being struck from all angles by twigs and branches that had been ripped from the trees. When we were about half way another cracking sound could be heard and we ran for our life not knowing where the tree was going to land but hoping it would not be on us. The tree fell behind us, smashing down and missing us by what seemed only inches. Eventually and thankfully we arrived at the sanctuary of my home and breathed a huge sigh of relief knowing that we were now although slightly battered and cut from the falling wood, safe.

It was not until morning however, when in the light of the autumn day we could see just how bad the damage had been. The telephone lines were down and there were many trees now floating in the lock cut. It looked like carnage but in comparison to how others fared we were lucky. Many lost their lives that night and we were thankful that all we suffered were a few mild scratches.

By the beginning of November we still had no house phone but other than that things began to return to normal save for the weir which would not be ready until 1991. I finished on the river and managed to get a job working for WH Smith in our local town. I had only been there for a couple of weeks before I had to take a day off but I had warned them in advance. This was the year of my eighteenth birthday and I was going to celebrate in style. My best friend and I caught the ferry to France and spent a long weekend seeing the delights of Paris. We visited the Louvre where we stood with what seemed like hundreds of Japanese tourists and surveyed the 'Mona Lisa.' Never have I been so disappointed with a painting. It was so small and so dark and I felt no positive emotion towards it at all. At the Pompidou Centre I laughed at what was supposed to be art, so ridiculous I found it but in the Musee D'Orsay I fell in love with the work of Rodin. On the day of my birthday we opened and drank Champagne on top of the Eifel Tower and so it was here in this stunning city that I developed a love for fine art and sculpture.

The trip out had been without incident but one could not say the same for the return journey. The crossing back was a little rough to say the least and made the majority of the passengers suffer with sea sickness. I have never suffered with any form of motion sickness but the stench of vomit that permeated the decks was enough to make anyone ill!

November rolled into December and there my memory begins to fade for the rest of this year. The first of December saw my mother once again fly out to Australia and her diary stops for this year half way through the month leaving me with no clues and therefore oblivious to the rest of the year.

Chapter 12 – 1988

In early spring my mother received a rapturous welcome home from
Australia but unfortunately it was short lived. It is evident by her
diary of this year that shortly after her return, the cracks of how dad
and I had lived over the past few months were beginning to show. It
is only by reading her diary of this year that the memories of how
1988 progressed came back to me. The house was a mess and it was
obvious to her that only the very basic of housework had been
completed. It was also not long before mum noticed that I was not a
happy young woman and in early March, just three weeks after her
return I told her a lot of what was wrong. I summed everything up in
just one sentence "I can't sleep and I cannot stand living here
anymore."   It was then that I explained in more detail.

I hadn't slept properly for weeks. It took forever for me to get to
sleep and when I did it was never for long. Something would always
wake me. I was either shouted at or, pushed, poked or prodded until I
woke up. The look on her face told me not to go into any more detail
about the bumps and bangs and items moving of their own accord in
my room. So then I told her why I hated living there and this she
understood completely. I loathed the mess. I hated not being able to
leave the island without having to use the new mode of transport.
The chaos caused by the work on the weir was such that our cars
were no longer able to cope with the mud and we had been given the
use of a dumper truck. If I wanted to go anywhere dad had to drive
me over the weir on this contraption and then I had to call him when
I was ready to come home so that he could come out and collect me.
Even on this machine I did not keep clean, my clothes became mud
stained to the extent where a lot of them had to be thrown out. I even
kept clothes just for this particular journey but it was not long before
they were ruined as well. I understood that in the grand scheme of
life people all over the planet had to endure far worse than we did
but that was not the point. As I understood it, every day brought
fresh incidents with the weir and these were now impacting both
mentally and physically on us. The problem was as mum put it, there
was nothing we could do except as she said, 'grin and bear it.'

My job with WH Smith came to an end and as there was nothing else on the horizon I went back to working on the river. I became Relief Lock Keeper covering not only Cookham Lock but Marlow Lock and Boulters in Maidenhead as well. It actually worked out quite well. If I was not at Cookham, Dad would give me a lift to either of the other locks in the morning and then in the evening I would simply beg a lift from the last boat owners that I was letting out at night.

Like most children I had no idea of the worry that I put my parents through. Even working away from the lock did not improve my mood. It was on the strong advice from a friend one evening at our local pub that I should seek help from my doctor and realizing that if even my friends had noticed my change in behavior I decided that it was worth a go.

I explained everything to the doctor. My mood swings, my insomnia and the reason for it, the fact that I was drinking too much and the fact that I was struggling to cope with what life was throwing at me. His answer was to put me on anti-depressants and to send me to a psychiatrist. It is true to say that the tablets helped but whether or not the psychiatrist had any effect is difficult to know as I was too scared to tell him about the 'others' that I shared our home with.
On March the nineteenth I made the decision to change bedrooms. Even though I had the larger room as a bed-sit I had still mainly continued to sleep in the smaller room. This decision was one that was not taken lightly as I was certain that I would be disturbed in this room as well but other than sleeping in the garden it seemed the only option. To my surprise I had the best night's sleep that I had had in months.

Towards the end of April I applied for a position with what was then the Department of Health and Social Security. It was a job I never expected to get and so was amazed when they sent me a date for an interview. I had asked dad what to expect and he told me that I would probably be interviewed by a couple of people and that they would want a very in depth interview. This, as it turned out was an understatement. On the day of the interview I was taken to a room which contained a large, long table with one seat prepared for me. On the other side of the table sat no less than twelve interviewers and I was overcome with absolute terror. How I got through the interview I shall never know as every answer I gave was either mumbled or I blabbered like a jittering idiot. It said a lot for this country's civil service because unbelievably they offered me the job. My starting salary, £4995.00!

It was this job that set in motion a series of events that were to change my life and bring me to where I am today but as my mother said back then 'you cannot make an omelette without breaking a few eggs.'

By now summer had arrived and with it came more problems than I ever imagined possible with the weir. The warm sunny days brought out the walkers who saw fit to ignore the various 'no entry' signs that we had put up around our garden.

One of my mother's more polite notices! It states 'Private. Walkers out of my garden + keep to your route.'

The Rambler's Association (although I am not quite sure when this happened) had petitioned Thames Water to open up the island to the public, something that we were all intently against. I still to this day do not understand this group's belief in the right to roam anywhere. They seemed ignorant and completely insensitive to our rights as a family and however bad it was it was about to get a whole lot worse.

It was because of their continual harassment that in the end drove me from Cookham Lock.

Because the weir gates had to be left open the 'happy' ramblers would wander through and treat the whole of the islands as if were one public park. It wasn't just the islands and the lock they treated in this way but our house as well.

One Saturday morning I was having a lie-in after a night out with my friends. I had come home by boat and had staggered into bed at maybe two or three in the morning. I therefore had no intention of waking up before lunch time. It was approximately eleven o'clock and I was deeply asleep when without warning I was shaken violently by the shoulders. I woke up to find a man in my room trying to ask me where the toilet was! I yelled at him to get the "Fuck out of my house," but at first he refused to go saying that all he wanted was the toilet. After a couple more expletives he left but the experience left me more than a little shook up not to mention bloody angry. This was not to be the first time that such an incident would occur.

This incident in my bedroom was one that I told my parents about and naturally they were not best pleased but there seemed little that they could do about it. I find it astounding now that such a situation could happen. If it was to happen in today's world arrests would be made, people would be charged and some may find themselves on the sex offenders register. Back then all we had was an apology. On another occasion I found a man in my parent's room and on two separate occasions I met with complete strangers coming up or down our stairs.

It was only when a different incident occurred that involved my mother that her anger really began to show. In our front garden we had two washing lines. One covered the width of the garden and the other just in front of it was a rotary line that was of an industrial size. On a beautiful, baking day in the summer my mother decided to wash all the blankets, sheets and pillow-cases. All of the washing was out on the lines by ten o'clock and took almost no time to dry. At lunch time she decided to bring it all in. The blankets were on the main line as she needed them to be higher to catch what small amount of breeze there was and the rest was hung out on the rotary. It was when she removed the first double sheet that she made her discovery. Crouching down behind the sheet was a man with obviously less manners than a dog going to the toilet. To say that my mother was incensed was putting it mildly and this man got the full force of my mother's wrath. She made him pick up his faeces with his bare hands and then sent him out of our garden yelling at him so that all around could hear exactly what he had done. The following week a similar incident occurred but this time the culprit was a woman. She received the same treatment.

Life was going from bad to worse. My mother wanted to leave but there was nowhere for her to go but she now told me that it was time I thought about getting out and getting away. The opportunity presented itself by way of work and ignoring the nagging feeling in the pit of my stomach I grasped the situation and by the end of the summer I had left.

I had become friendly with a guy at work and was soon introduced to his fiancé. We became good friends and when they invited me to live with them as a lodger saying 'no' did not cross my mind. They lived on the south coast in a spacious town house and at first we all got on very well. But somewhere along the line, and we were all to blame, it started to go horrendously wrong. It didn't help that I could not get a transfer and so I was travelling for six hours every day. We had to leave by four in the morning just to get to work on time and soon the novelty wore off. It would be unfair of me to go into too much detail about our relationship but by Christmas I wanted to leave and I am sure they felt the same. But I was too proud to admit that I had made a grave mistake and it was to be several weeks after the festive period before I realized that it wasn't just that I needed to leave but it was more of a case that I needed to escape.

Unfortunately, this was one Christmas that I could remember although I would have happily forgotten about most of it. The majority of the day had been fine and fairly pleasant but by the evening the arguments started up and I thought it best not to be there. In the dark and the cold I took myself for a walk not really realizing where I was going but knowing that I had to be anywhere but there. I found myself heading towards the beach. The sound of the waves in the distance although a cliché, seemed to call to me and for some reason I knew that at the water's edge I would be safe.

At some point I passed a night club and a man standing by its door wished me a 'Merry Christmas.' With tears running down my face I turned to him and said "For some," and continued walking. I have no idea how long I sat on the pebbled beach for, watching the waves in the moonlight and wondering if it was really worth carrying on but eventually I decided to leave, primarily because I was now so cold. I still had no intention of going back to the house and thought I would just wander round town until daylight but as I walked back past the night club that man that had spoken to me before was there and he asked me if I was all right? I told him I wasn't and thanked him for his concern and started to walk away but he called me back and invited me in. I told him I couldn't as I had no money but he said that it didn't matter. I hesitated, knowing that if I went in I could possibly be putting me in danger but he must have realized what I was thinking. The entrance where he was standing was to his office and he pointed out the security cameras, one of which showed his office on the monitor. Believing I had nothing to lose, I entered.

Immediately he found me a chair and then made a phone call up to the bar. He explained to the other person on the phone that I was there, distressed and slightly nervous and then asked them if they could bring down a drink for me. Putting the phone down he said that I could be reassured that I was safe and I believed him. Gently he asked me why was I on the beach alone on Christmas night and through tears I told him everything. We must of spoke for well over an hour and his kindness and hospitality I shall never forget. Eventuality I decided to leave and taking his advice about going back to the house because they would be worried about me I said thank you and wished him a Merry Christmas.

The road on which we lived was not residential. It mainly consisted of two types of businesses, antique shops and funeral directors. We lived next door to the latter. As I entered the street I was surprised to see that I was not the only one out walking at this time of night.

From the light of the street lamps I could see a smartly dressed gentleman, who I suppose may have been in his seventies, walking towards me although still some distance from me. As he came opposite to where I lived he stopped and crossed the street to about half way and then just stood there staring. I thought he must have been a friend of those I was staying with as I presumed he was looking towards our front door. I was just about to call out to him when he commenced walking again. But it was not to our front door he was heading but to the funeral parlour next door to us. I watched in curious disbelief as he walked right up to the parlour and then straight through the shop window disappearing as soon as he made contact with the glass. So there were ghosts even away from Cookham Lock, I mused.

As I suspected I had not been missed and took myself to bed without disturbing anyone. The rest of the week brought no further disruption and as we were all due to spend New Year with my parents at the lock I at last had something to look forward to.

New Year's Eve was an unmitigated disaster. My mother had invited some of her family to stay and unfortunately no one got along. The couple that I lived with had too much to drink and ended up arguing so much so that he walked or rather staggered out. My father sent me to look for him worried for his safety in case he fell into the river. Eventually I found him lurching far too close to the river bank above the lock and after some persuasion managed to bring him back to the lock house. I was more than glad to get to bed that night but made yet another mistake in my young nineteen years of life. I returned back to the south coast with them.

Chapter 13 – 1989

It is difficult to know how or where to start this chapter as my mother's diary and knowledge is of little use. For many years I have tried and mostly succeeded to block out the memories of the early part of this year so traumatic were they. At some point in January for reasons that I do not know as I was paying rent we were evicted from our home and ended up in bed and breakfast accommodation. We had no money and so I was unable to contact my parents and for a short while I suppose I could have been considered as 'missing.' The stress of travelling to and from work along with the stress of my living situation over the past few months had made me extremely ill. As a result of this I was suffering from headaches of the most severe which at best were sending me to bed but frequently were leaving me unconscious. The doctor I saw at the time suspected a tumor and put me on tablets until the necessary tests could be made. Unfortunately I had left the tablets in the house and was now unable to collect them.

My saving grace was that my Great Aunt lived fairly close to us and one day I finally admitted to myself that it was now time to go home. My Great Aunt lent me some money and on the second of February I arrived at Paddington station to be greeted by my mother and my mother's sister. My first stint at living away from home had finally and thankfully come to an end.

It was hard both mentally and physically to come to terms with what I had lived through but there was something in the near future to look forward to. Several of my friends were going travelling abroad and had asked me to join them. At first I had refused stating that I had a career but upon reflection I decided that at nineteen years old I did not want a career and agreed to accompany them to Israel.

As my employer's would not grant me a sabbatical I handed in my resignation and on the twenty-fifth (my lucky number) of April at nine-fifteen in the morning we flew out of Gatwick to land a few hours later at Tel-Aviv Airport. I had left London to the tunes on the radio appropriately of Elton John's 'Rocket Man' and John Denver's 'Leaving on a Jet Plane' under a blanket of grey cloud and heavy rain but touched down around lunch time to glorious, blistering sunshine. And so my adventure began.

Our destination was the Kibbutz Enzivan in the Golan Heights, the very north of the country and to get there we hired a car from the vicinity of the Airport. I was travelling with three others Daniel, who had been there before and two other friends Joanne and Sarah who like me were new to this strange and exotic, not to mention slightly dangerous land.

Daniel was sure he knew where he was going but as we drove further and further north it became clear that we were lost. After travelling for a couple of hours through barren and sun burnt countryside Sarah said that she was desperate for the toilet and we decided that as we could see a village through a fairly sparse group of olive trees in the distance we would stop there. Sarah could then relieve herself and we could find out exactly where we were.

Although the road was in fairly good order it was evident that as we drove into the village it was about the only thing that was. The village was deserted; the buildings just abandoned, crushed, bombed and shot out shells that were once home to a thriving community. Now, all they housed were rats and memories. This was our first visual confirmation that we had come to a country that had huge disputes with its neighbours. Sarah however, was still desperate for the toilet and as we exited the village Daniel pulled over so that she could hide behind a tree to relieve herself. As soon as she opened the door we could hear the distant barking of dogs and believed that as we could hear dogs we could not be too far from civilization. The barking grew nearer and nearer and the more clearly we could hear it so the more vicious and angry we realized it was. Just as Sarah got back into the car so a pack of wild, angry hounds set on us desperate to get to us through our mental confines. With the three of us more than encouraging him, Daniel drove off in a hurry!

A little while later it was a case of help finding us rather than the other way round as we were ordered to pull over by soldiers travelling in a jeep. Daniel got out to speak to them and soon returned with correct direction to our destination. It seemed we had strayed into Jordan!

A few hours later at around about tea time we eventually turned up
at the Kibbutz where we were allocated a chalet and work for the
foreseeable future. Our chalets were simple and consisted of two
beds, a shower room and a toilet, identical in fact to every other
chalet on the kibbutz. There must have been nearly thirty of these
small, boxed-like buildings in all and all sat to one side of a grassless
football pitch. Further up to the left were the main homes of those
whose community we now belonged to and their houses were far
more atheistically pleasing to the eye. But above us, towering into
the sky were the Golan Heights, with Syria seemingly almost a
touchable distance away.

There were many others already on the kibbutz and it was them that
gave us the 'low down' on the do's and do-not's of living in this
vicinity. They then showed the main essentials, where we went for
our meals, where the shop was and where we would find the night
club. We were told about the local village which had a bank as well
as a great bar and we were informed how to get there. You hitched to
the bus stop and then caught the bus. Hitching was also explained to
us. Never use your thumb, as in thumbing for a lift, which was
considered rude and an insult; always use your index finger pointing
downwards. Never get in a vehicle with a black number plate. This
would belong to an Arab and was considered very dangerous. Cars
with brown number plates were considered safe as these belonged to
the Hebrew community. Cars with blue number plates were also ok
as these were owned by the UN but they very rarely stopped for you.

Then there was the question of work. The work available for the
volunteers was varied and included working in the kitchen, the
orchards, the vineyard and the factory. There was no way I would
come all this way and end up working in doors so my first job out in
Israel was based in the orchards.

The orchards were a short drive away down roads that had not been
maintained and in the minibus in which we travelled we were
bumped and knocked as the driver maneuvered as best as he could
through the multitude of potholes. We would arrive in the orchard at

just after four the following morning and then start our intensive work. This consisted of walking the length of the line of trees and taking off any white leaves that we saw growing. Such hardship! Before we left we were given food for the morning and this we could eat when we wished. There was also water always available.

I was not working in the orchards for long, maybe for a few weeks when they moved us from the orchards to the vineyard. The job was the same but the danger was increased due to snakes that would curl up in the vines looking for shade from the heat of the sun. Although I found several I was never bitten. My most vivid memory of working on the vineyards was set forever early one morning. The sun, although barely risen, was already casting its Middle Eastern heat over this beautiful yet barren land. I had just come across several white leaves on an area of the vine when someone turned a radio on. The song 'More than a Feeling' by 'Boston' drifted over the sun scorched mountain side and down to where I was working. Whenever I hear that song it reminds me of how it complemented the peace and the warmth that I felt that morning.

Again, after a short while I was taken from this job and moved into the factory, a move I was not happy about but accepted gracefully. The factory made footwear. Wellingtons, riding boots and rubber jelly shoes, an eclectic mix to say the least. My job like a lot of us was to trim off the excess rubber from the jelly shoes. This was considered 'piece work' and as soon as you had fulfilled your quota you could leave for the day. It was not a job I enjoyed as I always seemed to be the last to leave.

The two female friends that I had travelled with were doing a similar job but Daniel was working on the factory floor working the machines that made the riding boots. One afternoon he approached me asking me if I would be interested in working on the machines? It seemed that they were short staffed and needed someone to run the 'jelly shoe' machine. Against my better judgment I said I would give it a try.

For the first time I entered the factory floor and met up with Daniel one sunny afternoon. The factory was a huge expanse with several large machines all busy churning out their goods. The machine that I was to work on was in the far corner and I felt daunted by my first sight of it. Stepping up onto a platform I could survey it in its entirety. It was circular in shape and from its central point approximately twelve jaw-like blocks protruded from it. The concept of how it worked was simple. At the back of the machine molten rubber was pumped into each jaw and so as the machine turned and each jaw would arrive where I was standing, it would open up revealing a hot, hardened, molded shoe. My job would be to remove the bung that had been created as a result of the rubber being pumped in, and then remove the shoe. The jaws would then close and continue round and the process would repeat again. The tricky bit was keeping up with the machine and at first I found it completely daunting but as time wore on I soon got the hang of it and found that I actually, for some strange reason enjoyed it. Within a couple of weeks I discovered that I could benefit from working on the machine. I would do a triple shift straight off at the beginning of each week and it would then leave me the rest of the week to do as I pleased.

My favourite time for working was at night. Then I had time to think and let my mind wander. Once in the rhythm of the machine there was no need to think about what you were doing and so my mind would turn to other thoughts, what was my family doing at home, what would I do when I went home, would I in fact, go home? The other reason to work nights was the spectacle in the morning. The east end of the factory held enormous double doors and every morning you could watch the sun rise. It was the most beautiful scene I had ever witnessed and gave me proof that however bad the night, light and hope would always conquer.

The factory was not without its dangers. Apparently most if not all of the machines had been condemned for at least ten years and this was readily obvious by the way the jaws on the machines would often open and close by themselves when the machines were switched off. Although a shock the first few times I witnessed it, I soon became used to the flattened cats and kittens that had crawled into the open jaws over the weekend when the factory was shut, only for the poor unsuspecting felines to become trapped when the jaws snapped back down on them.

It was not long before my friend's holiday had come to an end and it was time for them to leave me there. I was now more than at home in this environment and enjoyed my simple but beautiful lifestyle. One day whilst on my way to breakfast I noticed a poster near the entrance to the canteen and knew that if I did nothing else in Israel I would have to do this. The poster advertised a rock concert with not only one of my favourite artists but also the best guitar player in the world, Eric Clapton. Seizing the moment I immediately went to the office and booked my ticket. It seemed that I was not the only Clapton fan on the kibbutz and it was not long before we had a mini bus full.

The concert was to be held on the banks of the Sea of Galilee but expecting it to be a huge arena of sorts I did not take my camera. Oh, how I regretted this! There could have been no more than two thousand people there and we were so near the front I could almost have touched the stage.

The concert was fabulous. With the moon rising over the sea and the temperature still warm it was the most amazing experience. There was much hilarity at one point when a stray dog walked on stage and cocked its leg on a piece of equipment but the most memorable for me was when Mr Clapton played 'Wonderful Tonight." During the entire song a barn owl swooped low over the crowd. It was as if the bird was 'dancing' in the air to the music and it did not fly away until the song finished. It was obviously an owl of great taste.

Back on the kibbutz I was growing restless. The kibbutz was situated so far north that we could see Syria and just a short walk along the main road would take us to the Lebanese border. The Syrian Listening tower that was just beyond our compound, the variety of bomb shelters on the kibbutz, the Goren and the armed guards at the entrance of the Kibbutz was a constant reminder of exactly where I was. One morning, shortly after breakfast however, if those reminders were not enough, I was given another one. One that was to bring me face to face with the conflict that was engraved into the very fabric of this country.

By now my Hebrew language was almost fluent which proved a great asset working in the factory. The Druze in particular were grateful of someone else to speak to but it also helped me understand what the Jewish volunteers were saying particularly as they did not realize just how good my Hebrew had become! On a morning one day in July it may well have saved my life.

I had finished work at six and after a welcome breakfast of eggs, pancakes and several cups of tea I had retired back to my chalet for a well-earned rest. I loved this time of day as virtually everyone else was off the kibbutz and out on the fields working. After a shower I had changed into shorts and a t-shirt, collected my towel, sunglasses and alarm clock and had climbed onto our chalet roof to sleep. This was my normal place to sleep and with the alarm clock set to go off every hour I ensured I did not burn. I had just laid down, my head resting on my arms when I heard a noise. I sat up and looked around but at first I could not see anything but the sound was getting louder and closer. Then, from around the side of one of the mountains came a helicopter and it was heading this way. I watched with a feeling of growing apprehension as the helicopter began to descend. I could not believe it and as the realization that it was about to land on what could very loosely be described as our football pitch I moved, quickly. Not bothering to grab my belongings I made my way off the roof and scrambled back into the chalet.

When we first arrived at the kibbutz we were supposed to hand in our passports for security but for some reason I had never gotten around to it. Now, as I reached under my mattress for it I was glad. Through the shower window I could see that two men had exited the helicopter and were heading directly towards my chalet. Even through that small window I can still remember their guns glinting in the sunlight.

My door was smashed open and the two soldiers entered. One was tall and slim the other almost as broad as he was tall. The slim one never spoke as he checked the shower and toilet room and then waved his gun under my bed. Satisfied that I was alone, the soldiers turned their attention on me. The end of the barrel of one gun went firmly into my right temple; the others gun under my chin.

"What is your name," the burley one asked in perfect Hebrew.

"Rachel Andrews," I stammered (It is hard to talk with a gun in your chin) pushing my passport into their line of vision. "I am a British citizen."

The burley one barely looked at it and just threw it into the corner of the room. He then went on to ask if I had seen any strangers. I told him that I had not. They said that they were looking for an escaped prisoner and if I was harbouring him I would be in very bad trouble. I promised I was not and reiterated that I had not seen anyone that I did not know. At last, after an interrogation that must have lasted for at least half an hour, satisfied, they went to leave. As the burley one went to close the door behind him he turned back to me and in a perfect American accent he said "Have a nice day!"   I felt like throwing something large and heavy at him.

Through the open door I could see Ariel, our volunteer leader running towards the chalet. He burst in through the door and could not apologise enough for the incident. The reality of what had just happened now began to hit me and as this had to be reported and paperwork had to be filled out I followed him somewhat shakily up to his office. Sitting at his desk he poured me a tremendous glass of vodka. Sipping at the welcome drink I stole a look at his clock and was amazed to see that it was nearly ten o'clock.

News of this incident travelled faster than a bullet around the kibbutz and all day people came to see if I was all right. So concerned were some of my friends that they decided to take me out to the bar that evening. We hitched down to the bus stop on a lorry carrying chickens to wait for the bus which was due at any moment. It soon became apparent that all was not well in the vicinity. There seemed to be an immense amount of flies buzzing about. After an irritating minute or so flapping our arms around believing that an animal must have died, just as the bus arrived, I had a look round the back of the bus stop. I told no-one of what I saw. Apparently much of the land in the area was mined but there is a stretch of land between the roads and the common land that is clear of land mines. This was called no-man's land. As the others trooped onto the bus I found the cause of all the flies and will never forget that sight. The drink at the bar was one of the most needed that I ever had but it was also to be my last there. This whole incident told me that it was time to leave the kibbutz and explore a little more of Israel before I went home.

A few days later I and another girl left the kibbutz and headed south towards Jerusalem. The trip was taken in a comfortable air conditioned bus and to my amazement cost only 96 pence (I cannot remember the price in shekels.) We found a hostel in the walls of the north of the city near the main gate and used this as our base for exploring. I woke the following morning in a room of white washed walls to the sound of the city calling the inhabitants to prayer. It was a sound I will never forget. The chanting and the bells could not have changed since the days of Jesus himself. It was deeply relaxing but also invigorating and moving at the same time.

I could not begin exploring however, until I had fulfilled a promise. A couple of days before I had left the kibbutz a young man called Ravi who worked in the factory had approached me requesting a favour. He asked me if I could deliver a package for him once I arrived in Jerusalem. Feeling slightly unnerved by his request I asked for more details of this package. He smiled at me, told me to "stay there" and scurried off returning a few minutes later with the parcel in question. He handed it to me and asked me to open it. I did and was surprised to see that it contained a fairly large quantity of money. "It is my wages," he explained. "I want you to take it to my family. As you are going near their home it will save me spending money to go and see them. Will you do this for me please?"
"Of course I will," I answered. "Tell me their address."

Ravi's family lived in a block of flats at the far end of the town and if I am honest when I arrived there I was a little apprehensive. The area looked a little rough around the edges and reminded me of a council estate back home. I followed his directions to the second or third floor (I cannot remember precisely) of a block of run down looking flats and it was not long before I was knocking on his family's door. Ravi must have telephoned ahead to let me know that I was coming to see them because as soon as the door opened there were great cheers and shouts of "Welcome!   Welcome Rachel!"   I was enthusiastically shown into the flat by Ravi's mother.

I was led into a fairly spacious lounge and offered a seat and a cup of tea which I politely accepted whilst handing over the money to Ravi's mum. Then I was shown around the flat and introduced to all the members of his family. Other than his mother I met his Nan and granddad, his sister and her two young children and also his younger brother. I was told that his father, his older brother and his brother-in-law were at work. That meant that there were nine people living in this flat and it was only two bedrooms. They showed me how they managed; beds could be pulled out of walls, the coffee table in the lounge was turned upside down at night and became a cot/bed for the children and the sofa also converted. I was amazed. All of these people lived in this tiny apartment and all appeared happy and content. Back home there would be nothing but complaints to social services but here they looked after each other and all seemed to love having each other around.

Ravi's mum asked me to stay for lunch but I politely refused saying that I had arranged to meet the girl I was travelling with and she would be worried if I did not turn up. Although this was true I was actually more concerned about being another mouth to feed and so after an hour of their fabulous company I said my goodbyes and left. I found this such a heart-warming contrast to the meeting with the two soldiers less than a week before.

Using the hostel as a base we took trips to all the main tourist attractions in and around Jerusalem. On the Mount of Olives I got into a spot of grief and was nearly kidnapped for marriage! My 'husband-to-be' was more than happy to send my father two hundred and fifty camels as payment for me. A payment I was later to find out was exceptionally good but I managed to get out of the situation my telling a small white lie and saying that I was already betrothed to another man! A trip to Bethlehem was to leave me saddened. The bible tells that Jesus was born in a stable and had humble beginnings. The birth place of Jesus is now marked in a small room in a church. The walls are adorned with paintings that must be priceless and as to his actual birth place? The floor is painted in gold leaf and is almost repulsive in its splendor.

There was one pilgrimage that I felt I had to make, the Yad Vashem. This is a place of remembrance to all those who lost their lives in the holocaust. Maybe it is because my name is Jewish or maybe it was because of all the films and history programs I had seen over the years but for some reason I felt compelled to go. I arrived at the gates and walked the long path towards the museum. On either side of me hundreds of trees grew and it was only on closer examination I realized the significance. Each tree represented someone who had died in the atrocity. Inside the building there were more heart rendering tributes. A single candle flickered in a large room. Surrounding the candle were many mirrors reflecting the single flame until the whole room seemed to be filled with a million little lights. Each was a reflection, an effigy of someone who had lost their lives. In another room, a pile of thousands of children's shoes, all that was left after the German army had completed their ethnic cleansing. I left the Yad Vashem with a greater understanding of how the Jewish population had suffered during the Second World War and had felt deeply moved and humbled by the experience.

Towards the end of July I made the decision to return home to England. I had run out of money and was now homesick. I made a reverse call home and let my parents know that I would be home by the end of the month but things did not go according to plan. I had saved enough money for a stand-by flight home and enough to pay for transport from the airport to my house but the flight I intended to take was full. I went to a youth hostel in Tel Aviv and explained my predicament. They said I could sleep on their roof for no charge as long as I helped out in the kitchen to pay for my stay and as the next available flight was not for several days I had no choice. For three extra days I enjoyed the warmth and hospitality of Tel Aviv sleeping al fresco in the warm night air.

I met up with a traveler called Dave who was due to take the same flight at me and on the day we were due to leave we caught the bus together to the airport. I was already imagining my home coming as I walked into the terminal. Wearing nothing more than a swimsuit, shorts, t-shirt and jelly shoes and sporting a rucksack on my back I did not realize just how scruffy I looked and was surprised when a customs officer called me over. In what was to turn into a humiliating experience my bag was taken and thoroughly examined to the point where they put cameras down the metal structure of my bag. Satisfied that my bag did not contain any drugs or other illegal substances they now turned their attention on me. I was taken to a small cubicle and an apologetic medical examiner asked me the inevitable, "Could I please bend over?"

Needless to say I was the last on the plane and as I made my way to my seat that was next to Dave's I could feel every pair of eyes staring at me. However, I was just glad to be on board. Once we were in the air a gentleman no older than forty but with the whitest blondest hair, and the bluest eyes that I have ever seen who was sitting behind us tapped me on the shoulder and asked if I was ok? I smiled weakly and told him it wasn't an experience I wanted to repeat!   He then proceeded to call a stewardess and ordered both me and Dave some cans of lager. I was very grateful for his kindness.

On August forth we touched down at Gatwick somewhere around lunch time and I worked out the best way home was to get a train to Victoria and then a tube to Paddington and then another train to Maidenhead. Once in Maidenhead I could work out how to get home from there.

I must have looked like a complete idiot on the journey to Victoria. I shared the carriage with a few other people which mainly consisted of a family with young children. As soon as we left the confines of the airport I became hysterical with excitement. There was something out of the train window which I had forgotten all about. It was the colour green which is sadly lacking in Israel. The terrain of Israel is predominately barren and very little grows on the ground. The sunbaked soil is evident all over the country and so without realizing it I had become used to seeing a mainly sandy-brown and forlorn landscape. Now back in England I felt overwhelmed with the sight of lush green fields full of lush green grass with lush green trees that seemed to be everywhere and I happily suffered a sensory overload. I did not know which window to look out of and charged from one side of the carriage to another in rapturous pleasure. At one point I noticed a couple looking at me rather peculiarly and in answer to their odd expressions all I could say to them was "Green!" in a high pitched, childlike voice.

Once at Paddington I caught the train back to Maidenhead and from there I rang my father. It dawned on me that I should have been home days ago and I realized that they would have been very worried about me. My mother's diary bears this out. My father answered the phone with his usual deep voice "Cookham Lock?"
"It's me," I answered. "Can you come and collect me please?"
"Where are you?"
"Maidenhead station," I replied.
"I'm on my way."

He must have driven like a madman as it was only a few minutes later when I saw his red pick-up truck drive along the road towards the station. I saw him park his car and as he walked towards me he had the biggest grin on his face that I had ever seen before or since. I thought that for the first time he was going to give me a hug but as soon as he was close enough to grab my bag from me his face changed and in mock seriousness he said "Why didn't you call me from the airport?" The moment had gone.

When we arrived home he told me to stay outside and I heard him say to my mum who was in the lounge "There's a parcel for you outside."
When she saw me she broke down in tears and then paraded me round the lock-side as if I had returned like the prodigal son. Knowingly my father had busied himself making me a cup of tea and a bacon sandwich. It was good to be home.

After a couple of weeks getting back into lock life it was time for me to find a job. This I did with relative ease but not before a letter had arrived for me from the Home Office. When I opened and read it I was not sure whether to laugh or cry such were the contents. The letter stated that as I was in this country illegally I should make arrangements to leave immediately or I would be deported! My father took up my cause and after a few choice words on the telephone to the Home Office where he told them to check their records which would show them not only where I was born but also who I had recently worked for before I went to Israel, they decided to let me stay. I thought it was very kind of them!

Finding a job proved to be no problem and so working all week for a satellite installation company aptly called Startreck and being out with friends most evenings it kept me away from the house and the lock. The weir situation had barely improved and the continual harassment from the walkers and the members of the public was still causing us problems. On the seventeenth September the rambler's association decided to prove a point by sending fifty of their delightful members to the island by boat. Even as a nineteen year old I thought that this was petulant. Walks around the islands often now meant taking a carrier bag to collect the litter that they left behind, a problem that we never had with the boaters. I began to wonder why I ever went away or whether I should have come home.

For many weeks after my return the upstairs had remained quiet with no activity. I am not sure when it began again but I remember it was before my birthday. I was lying on my bed reading when I heard someone cough. Thinking someone had come into my room I had looked up but there was no one there so I carried on with my book. The next instance I was hit on the head as another book flew across the room and landed on my bed beside me. It seemed that I could not get peace anywhere and even ignoring it didn't make it go away. Although there was nothing as serious as being assaulted by a phantom book thrower for the rest of the year small incidents did continue to occur. Things would go missing and then reappear in odd places, I would find items moved slightly as if someone did not like where or how I had placed them and when I would enter the bedroom I would often find my bed linen heaped untidily on the floor.

Save for my birthday party in November, the rest of the year was uneventful. I had invited a 'few' friends to the house as my parents were on holiday in Gibraltar. The problem was that as we all congregated at my local pub. I had friends coming who I had met in Israel and it was easier for them to find the pub rather than find our house. Whilst in the pub our conversations were overheard and later, while the party was in full swing we ended up with fifty or so gate crashers. It would not have been a problem as we had locked the weir gates but a boating club were, unbeknown to me, also having a party on our island and they had left the gates unlocked. It resulted in me needing to call the police. The police must have heard about the party as well as they not only turned up in full force but also very, very quickly. It turned out that they were waiting in the area just in case. Along with several police cars and a riot van an ambulance and fire engine turned up as well. They took away all those I did not know and the party carried on into the wee small hours. Luckily the house suffered very little damage and a car which I later found out was balancing precariously over the river by the weir, (the driver had lost the road) was pulled to safety.

The rest of the year flew by very quickly. Christmas was spent at home and much improved on the previous year. Friends and I all came together in the evening and celebrated at our local pub in style. As the year came to a close I knew that so had a chapter in my life. I looked forward to the following year with a new sense of optimism and wonderment.

Chapter 14 – 1990

This year came in quietly but unfortunately as a wolf steals up on a flock of unsuspecting sheep the peace did not last for long. The weather became very rough with high winds and heavy rain which at one point was so severe that a lot of the inhabitants of Maidenhead, particularly near the river, had to be evacuated. This weather hampered my journey to and from work. Although I was still working for the same company I was now, along with several others, located in Windsor. Thankfully the company had provided us with a mini bus so at least our travel expenses were taken care of.

The weather was causing havoc and the effects were being felt at the lock. Our electricity had been knocked out and we were without power for well over a week. It made living particularly difficult especially as we had a young guest. A friend of mine had two small children and the younger of the two was staying with us while his mother worked away. Jamie was just a baby, I think not even a year old and my mother was doing her best to care for him. With no running water and no heating life was rather difficult. Combine that with the horrendous conditions on the weir it was becoming unbearable. The dumper truck had now been replaced by a tractor and was our only way on and of the islands and at one point during the first month of the year even the tractor could not cope with the conditions.

The evening of the twenty-fifth of January will stay in my mind forever. In torrential rain and heavy winds I had left work at just after five in the evening. The mini bus was full and my colleagues and I were all in high spirits. On the way out of Windsor, just passed the sports centre I saw a body lying on the rain soaked pavement. Yelling at the driver to stop we pulled over and went to see if we could help. The man was lying flat on his back and dressed in sports-wear. I presumed he had only recently left the sports centre but however long he had been lying there; he was showing no signs of life. I was one of the youngest in our group but it soon became apparent that no one knew any basic or otherwise live saving techniques. One girl who was younger than me became distressed and I saw no alternative but to do what I could. Kneeling down in the rain by the side of the man I felt for his pulse but could find none. Above the noise of the wind and rain I screamed out for someone to call an ambulance and the young girl then began sobbing begging me for him not to be dead. I felt I had no choice but to begin mouth to mouth and heart massage. At some point two other people turned up who were from the sports centre and brought with them some basic breathing apparatus but it was incomplete and therefore did not work and so I continued the lifesaving procedure.

I have never worked so hard in my life for nothing. I knew this man had already died but also knew that the people surrounding me expected me to do something. It is the strangest and the most unsettling feeling to know that you are forcing your living breath into a dead man's lungs. I continued for many minutes until the ambulance eventually turned up and as they took over and laid him on a stretcher I spoke quietly to one of the paramedics explaining that he had died before we had even arrived. We returned to the mini bus and continued our journey but the high spirits had evaporated and had been replaced by melancholy and the gentle sobbing of my young female colleague.

Dad had gone out and I had to make my way over the weir by foot as dad had the keys for the tractor with him. This small journey showed me in no uncertain terms why we used the tractor. The conditions were so bad they beggared belief. By the time I arrived home I was entirely caked in mud after having lost my footing several times and was also freezing cold. At one point I had slipped down the bank and had come so close to falling in that one of my feet had actually got wet in the river. I only managed to save myself by grapping hold of a length of rope that was attached to a generator. I arrived through the front door to find mum bathing the baby by candlelight and without a word to her or bothering to change I took the brandy from the cupboard and filled a glass. It took me less time to drink the contents than it did to pour it.

Our home was not a happy one. The relationship between my parents was at an all-time low and for the first time by reading my mother's diaries I have since discovered just how bad it really was. It appears that the arguments had turned violent and my father's drinking was now badly out of control. Things were no better on the paranormal side either. A comment in my mother's diary on the seventh of March retrieved a memory that I had long forgotten. My mother states that I had requested that we put all our make-up in the spare room which to anyone would be considered an odd request especially as I refused to give a reason. When I first read it, like a drain backing up bubbling with dirty, muddy water, the memory and reasons for the request came back to me. The spirits had started dabbling in graffiti and making a mess with more than just my bed clothes.

At first I had barely noticed the tiny lip stick smudges on my mirrors or the slightly smeared blotches on one of my photos. It took me several weeks to see the smudge of red grease that had been badly applied to the nose of an ornament. It was actually a blob of lipstick that had been pushed into the carpet that first caught my attention. I had stood on it without realizing and it was not until I saw the red on my foot and wondered where on earth it had come from did I realize that something else was occurring.

I went around all of the upstairs rooms and cleaned up what I found. It was not just lipstick that the spirits had taken to using; it was eye shadow as well. I found grey shadow on one of my teddies and a dusky green colour on another. At first I thought, hoped that it could have been the baby but he had gone back to his mother several weeks before and certainly the lipstick was fresh; I would have noticed it otherwise. I remember sitting on my bed and crying. I did not understand and had no idea of where to go for help. Why would complete strangers believe me if my own family had refused to believe me so many years before?

By April things began to calm down. The weather had improved and my parents were trying harder to get along but again the image of the wolf creeping towards the sheep comes to mind as at the beginning of April the company that I worked for announced that it was bankrupt. Although my job was safe for the foreseeable future as it was being taken over the uncertainty of knowing that I would have to find a new career niggled at the back of my mind for many months to come.

The need to once again escape from the lock was bearing down on me and refuge came in the form of a couple of girls that I worked with. We decided to rent a house together in Windsor and by the end of the summer I had moved out.

Life at Windsor was good and I felt like a typical twenty year old. The company was taken over by a major satellite company and I had been given a promotion. It is strange to think that back then I earned more money than I have ever done before or since. So for some time I lived the high life. I was out almost every night, spending far too much time in any one of the many pubs and wine bars that Windsor has to offer. I found myself a boyfriend who happened to be in the army and generally had a good time. Although I still visited my parents on a regular basis the stress levels had all but diminished.

The house thankfully seemed devoid of paranormal activity although I am sure it was old enough to have a history that would have been worth discovering. It was built over two stories with three bedrooms and a bathroom on the top floor, the lounge and kitchen on the first floor and a bedroom with en suite on the ground floor. I found it reassuring to realise that when I left something lying around, it was still there when I needed it next.

There were two incidents that happened within the house and garden although not of a spooky nature is worth mentioning. The first concerned money. My bedroom was on the ground floor and had its own shower room which made getting ready for work each morning, very easy. By the side of my bed I had a large jar that all my change went into. There was never less than eighty pounds in it but after a few weeks I noticed that the amount in the jar never went up and indeed seemed to go down all of its own accord. I began to keep a regular check on the value of its contents and when I had enough evidence to show what I already knew, that I was being robbed from right under my nose I approached the rest of my house mates.

I called a meeting one evening in our lounge and told all three of them to sit on the sofa. So that I could not be accused of 'looking at anyone the wrong way' I turned by back to them and began telling them of my findings. We all loved a good mystery and so I took on the persona of an investigating officer. "One of you is a thief," I commenced in a dramatic tone, "And I cannot abide thieves. I thought we were friends so if one of you needs money then why haven't you asked?   So the deal is this. I will give you one week to return the money from whence it came or I shall go to the police. I have already spoken to a friend of mine who is on the river section and he is more than happy to investigate. You see, the money has gone from my jar and therefore only mine and the perpetrators fingerprints will be on that jar. So it will be easy for the policeman to ascertain which one of you is stealing from me." After a brief pause I turned round to them and said "Anyone want a cup of tea?"

The truth of the matter was that I had not asked any member of the police force to investigate if necessary for me but my gamble paid off. Within a couple of days the money was paid back and a note of apology was left by the side of my bed. My money was never stolen again.

The second incident that occurred actually happened in our 'compact and bijou' garden. A couple of us decided that it needed a tidy and a good weeding and one Saturday we set about our task. The garden consisted of a small patch of grass, a rotary washing line and a small area of shrubs at the far end. The whole area could not have been more than twelve foot square.

We decided to clear out the rubbish which mainly consisted of dead, rotting leaves and stinging nettles and it was while we were clearing the leaves from around the shrubs that we made our discovery. Under the hydrangea I found a plastic bag. That in itself was nothing unusual. It was the contents that gave us cause for concern and if I am honest, we panicked. The bag contained a bone. A largish type bone; a largish, arm shaped bone. My friend and I looked at each other. At first I firmly believed that it certainly was not a bone that once belonged to any farm animal. Through the plastic bag we studied it, turning it over to look at it from different angles and then before I had a chance to speak my friend was digging in the soil. "What are you doing," I enquired rather bemused? "Digging a hole so that we can bury it," she replied. "I don't care who or what it may have belonged to but I don't like it"

"Shouldn't we take it to the police," I asked. "That is what we should do?"

"If we do that and it is human they will come and dig all of this up and the landlord will go crazy. We will be homeless. I don't know about you but I have nowhere else to go."

We never did go to the police. The thought of having to go home again was not a thought I relished. So I left her to deal with the bone as she saw fit. But I did do something about it. Unbeknown to the rest of the girls I dug the bone up and took it to the local butchers. I left the butchers more than a little relieved. The bone was porcine. However, here I must confess that I never relayed this information to my housemates. The thought of them thinking that we lived with human remains was rather amusing to me at the time.

Unfortunately going home soon became the only option. For reasons that I did not understand then and cannot remember now the company that I worked for became embroiled in more financial difficulties. Wages stopped being paid into our accounts and very senior members of staff became suddenly unavailable. No matter what problems we were having our landlord still needed his rent. This was the only time in my life that I ever owned a credit card. I had to use it to keep a roof over my head but when it became apparent that there would be no more wages I took on the persona of the rat and jumped ship just as quick as I could. Home, then became the only option. The balance on the card by this time was very much in the red and my father was more than willing to pay it off just so long as I paid it back just as soon as I could.

It was now autumn and my life was all a bit of a mess. I had no job and no immediate prospect of getting one but as always the optimist I knew that life had to improve. November helped me to turn twenty one and as a birthday present my mother was due to take me to Australia in the New Year. I knew that there was no point in even searching for a job until after I returned so settled down to another six weeks of living at Cookham Lock.

Chapter 15 – 1991

On a bitterly cold morning in early January a Bowing 747 took off from Luton Airport bound for Perth, Western Australia. On board my mother and I looked out of the window glad to be leaving the English Winter behind.

After a stop off in Singapore my mother gave me some words of warning about her sister and two sons that we were going to be spending the next six weeks with. The one piece of advice that I remember was not to swear as Aunty Carol didn't swear and hated it. Many hours later we touched down in Perth a little after lunch time and before retrieving our bags we headed to the ladies toilet to refresh and make ourselves look a little more human and a little less jet-lagged. My mother's advice went out of the window as soon as we entered the arrival lounge and I set eyes upon my cousins. I had not seen them since I was a young child and they were small scrawny brats. "Bloody Hell," I exclaimed! "What the Hell do they feed you out here?" My two cousins were just millimeters of seven foot tall and left their mother looking almost dwarf like in their presence. As soon as I had realized my faux-par, mainly because my mother had jabbed me in the ribs, I apologized but my aunt and cousins just laughed and hugged us.

My Aunt's house was and is situated in a small estate just outside Perth called Beldon and so thankfully the journey to a comfy seat and a decent meal was not far away. However, within minutes of sitting down to a light meal I had regressed to a child and literally fell asleep in my meal. My head hit the plate and it was only the sound of laughter that woke me up. Unable to stay awake I headed for our room and slept for several hours.

My holiday was to be a relaxing combination of sight-seeing and gentle adventure. I wanted to explore the country and with the advantage of having cousins who had more than enough local knowledge, I knew I would be in for some treats that the average tourist might not necessarily experience. Of course, Australia is an enormous place and I knew that I would only see a small part of it.

I became particularly close to Gary, the youngest of the two brothers partly because we were closer in age but mainly because we both shared a love for wildlife although if I am honest his love covered more species than mine.

A few days after our arrival Gary suggested that we get up early the following morning and he would take me to see some 'twenty-two's.' The perplexed look on my face told him that I had no idea what he was talking about and so he explained that this was the Ausi name for a type of parrot. Getting up at four the following morning was not something I relished but nevertheless readily agreed to as the thought of seeing some Australian wildlife while others slumbered, appealed to me.

That night I went to bed early and duly set my alarm for the appointed time. I awoke to warm sunshine and without disturbing my mother I went in search of a cup of tea and a shower. Carol's house is a typical Australian property. It is a bungalow style with three bedrooms. As there was no room in the house for us to sleep friends had lent her a caravan which was positioned in her car port. We entered the house from the side door which opened up into a sun room. From the sun room we walked into an open plan lounge and dining room with the kitchen at the far end. To the left of the kitchen was a hall way which led to the bathroom and three bedrooms. The plan was to make tea and wake Gary.

I have taken time to describe the layout of the house so as to explain why I had no intention of walking to Gary's room and waking him. Still half asleep I had put the kettle on to boil before my attention was drawn to a shadow above the hall door. I don't like spiders, small British house spiders terrify me so my reaction to what was sitting, staring at me was more than understandable. I screamed and dropped the cup. The Bird Eating spider, the size of a dinner plate didn't flinch and for that matter neither did anybody else in the house. I was alone with this enormously hairy, eight-legged monster.

Once I had more control of my senses I formulated a plan to wake Gary without having to go near the horrifically furry beast and praying that spiders couldn't fly or jump fifteen or so feet I climbed over the breakfast bar that separated the kitchen from the dining area and retracing my steps went back outside, around to the front of the house and banged on his window. After a few moments I managed to wake the sleeping beauty up and warned him of the unwelcome guest in his house. To my utter horror when I was back inside I found him picking the spider up and popping it into a glass jar. It then transpired that he collected spiders although once he had caught them they did not live for very long. He showed me, to my disgust, a large pin board which held his examples of Australian Arachnids. Needless to say I was not impressed.

The rest of the morning did improve greatly. We left the house just before five and drove to a beautiful area several miles away. The area was on the edge of the bush and consisted of many trees and grassland. Once there Gary gave me some bird seed and instructed me to stand near the trees and hold out my arms. I did so and almost immediately the image of the spider was wiped from my mind. Stunning green parrots flew down and landed on my arms, shoulders and head. They politely took it in turns to eat the seed from my hands and I was astounded at their confidence with the human race. This spectacle, I was informed, was local knowledge only.

Just off the coast of Freemantle is a small island called 'Rottnest Island' or 'Rotto' as it is locally known and my aunt suggested that it was worth a visit. It had some small furry creatures that I might find interesting. We took a boat over and stepped onto what I could only describe as paradise. This island is lapped by warm seas and has the most stunning coast-line that I have ever seen anywhere. The small furry creatures were not hard to spot either. The island was originally named by Dutch sailors who named it after the Quokkas that they found there. Rottnest apparently translates as Rat-nest and it was not hard to understand why. Quokkas are like very small wallabies and have a rat-like resemblance. It is thought that they are a result of a cross between the two and knowing that this country holds some of the strangest animals on the planet it would not surprise me.

My trip to this island was severely hampered by the fact that at some point earlier (I cannot remember when) I had sprained my ankle and found walking virtually impossible. Gary and I decided that once my foot had healed we would return for a better exploration.

The following week we landed at the island this time complete with sleeping bags and wash kits as we were planning to stay the night. A small area of the island had been turned over to a camp site with the tents already erected. However, before entering them I made Gary check the interior for any sign of eight legged and/or poisonous life! Once satisfied that all was clear we changed into our swimming costumes, grabbed our towels, snorkels, sunglasses and sun-cream and leaving the rest of our kit in the tent, went off to explore.

A little way along from the site we found a small but beautiful natural pool. There were several people around but this seemed like a good place to snorkel. The pool was only waste deep but the water was almost hot and crystal clear. At the far end it opened up and seemed to lead to the shallows surrounding the island.

A photo of the pool in question

As I entered the pool with Gary I overheard a large, obnoxious, American man in brown check swimming trunks say "Gee, there isn't much to see around here is there?" to anyone that may have been listening. I was astounded and wondered if he was suffering from temporary sun-blindness or more likely, permanent ignorance. I concluded it was the latter once I had entered the pool, placed my snorkel and mask on and looked under water. For there, swimming unhindered, were large, glistening silver in the sunlight, fish. I am not sure what make or model they were but they must have each weighed many pounds and were stunning to look at.

Gary and I however, were off to explore further afield. If I remember correctly, once outside of the pool he went to the left and I to the right. The pool opened up into a serious of deeper pools all surrounded by deep forests of thick kelp swaying hypnotically in the gentle ebb and flow of the waves. I noticed movement to my right and was delighted to see a small clown fish darting in and out of the shelf that edged the area of this pool. Entranced by its colours and knowing it would be a better guide than any human I began to follow it. It led me for some time through other pools and in and out of kelp and other underwater greenery. Occasionally I would stop and look up to make sure I was not going out too deep but this fish seemed to prefer the shallows although I had long since been able to touch the bottom without diving down.

Then after many minutes and without warning the fish shot off and disappeared into the safety of some coral and I found myself in a deep pool completely surrounded by kelp. The sun glinted through the water casting shadows on the sea bed which although was many feet below was still perfectly visible. It was then that I felt the atmosphere change and that little voice inside my head told me to get the hell out of there. Beginning to panic I looked around but could see nothing. I was in no doubt however, that something in amongst the kelp but just beyond my vision could see me. I followed the clown fish's advice and swam towards the rough shelf of rocks and coral and hauled myself up. Looking around I saw that there was nowhere for me to go except back the way I had come. If I walked across the rocks I was likely to cut my feet and that was one thing I did not want to do. I had seen 'Jaws' and much as I like and respect sharks I knew that if my blood entered the water they would not have the same feelings towards me.

Going back into the water I took another look around but could still see no other signs of life. I hoped that whatever it was had swam off but I was taking no chances. Carefully and actually hearing my heart pounding in my chest I half crawled and half swam back, keeping as close to the rock shelf as possible until I was close enough to pull myself into shallower waters. Not too far away I could see Gary looking for me and so I waved to him and indicated that I was heading back to dry land. I never saw what was behind the kelp but I know there was something there. Whatever it was could have been harmless and may have just been curious but I knew deep down that I should not have hung around to find out.

It transpired that this day turned out to be the hottest on record for Australia and we spent the rest of the afternoon sitting under a Eucalyptus tree in the court yard of a tavern sipping ice cold Australian lager which tastes completely different to the weak, fizzy liquid that we consume in the UK, eating pizza and feeding tit-bits to the rather pretty but flea invested quokkas. Later, as the day came to an end Gary advised me that if I was to clean my teeth and go to the toilet at the near-by shower blocks I should go before dark. "Things come out at night," he said.

The following day before we caught the boat back to the mainland we explored the rest of the island by foot. We saw more quokkas, beautifully stunning birds and richly coloured, decadent flowers. It was strange to think that back home we would pay a fortune for some of those blooms but there they were growing wild and free.

Another trip a week or so later was to prove equally as memorable but unfortunately on that occasion my sixth sense was to let me down. My Aunt's boyfriend owned a Trimaran and he agreed to take us out to Penguin Island for the day. My mother, who although has lived by water for a considerable part of her life does not like boats and did not wish to accompany us so we left her behind and set off for another adventure.

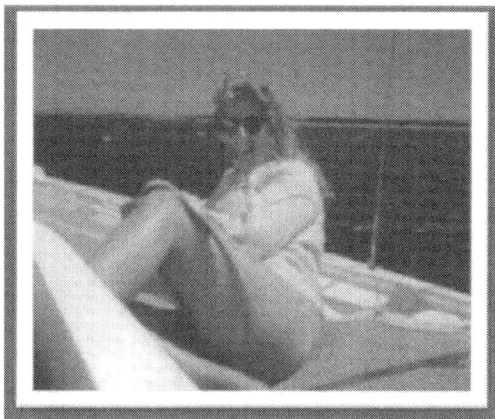

Lapping up the sun on the Trimaran

We arrived mid-morning and laid anchor just off the beach and although I was met once again with a stunning view I was saddened to see or rather not see any penguins. What I did see in the distance however was something very large lying at the water's edge but I could not see what they were. We stepped off the boat and waded to shore. Walking further along the beach the creatures at the edge of the water became clear to me. Huge sea-lions sunbathed, completely ignoring the other people that were standing only a few feet away from them taking photos. I too joined in and took some lovely shots and only returned back to the boat when it was time for lunch.

After a meal of salad, cheese and wine we sunbathed for a while before I decided to go and see what I could discover under water. Here there was no kelp, just a mass of white sand and clear blue water. There were other boats around, many with RIBS and so I knew that if danger did approach, help would not be too far in coming.

Making a point of going no further out than the boats were moored I found huge crabs and more stunning fish of various sizes. I was not too far from our boat and fairly deep under water when I heard muffled shouts from my aunt. I looked around but could see nothing to worry about and so believing that another boat must have been on the move I swum down deeper to avoid its propeller. For a few short moments the sun was blocked out from above as the boat passed over and once it had gone I rose to the surface.

"Did you see it," called my aunt?

"The boat?   No, not really," I answered. My aunt looked confused. "What Boat?   There wasn't a boat. There was a massive manta ray that swam over you. It must have had a wing span of at least twelve feet. Don't tell me you missed it?"

I could not believe it. One of the most beautiful fish in the ocean, not to mention the most graceful had swum within inches of me and I was looking the other way. Typical!

At around three o'clock every day there is a wind that blows in off the sea onto the mainland called the Freemantle Doctor. That time was soon approaching and we had to leave before it came in. Unfortunately we left it a little late and just as we were about to depart so it hit us. We had weighed anchor and were heading out to sea but the Freemantle Doctor had other ideas and hit us broadside. Our boat was caught in its grip and started heading for a reef that protruded out of the water. My aunt's boyfriend was more than a little worried as if we hit the reef it would smash the boat to pieces. "You have to get out of the boat and turn us around," he shouted urgently to me as he tried to maneuver the boat against the wind. The others were all involved with the sails and the rigging and so it was down to me.

I jumped out of the boat in to shoulder high water and heaved the boat round so that we were pointing in the right direction. Vincent and Gary pulled at the sails and at the right time Don yelled at me to get back on board. Feeling my adrenaline coursing through me I gave the final push and the boat began to move at speed away from the reef. I leapt out of the water and onto the boat with the ease and grace of an athlete!   To this day I have no idea how I did it!

The rest of the holiday was taken up with more trips out to sea, visits to local animal parks, a look around Perth, the celebration of Australia Day and regular trips to Hilary's. This was a large shopping complex and quay that was not only beautiful and up-market but also served the most amazing cheese cake that I have ever tasted. It also housed safe swimming in its harbor. That is of course, except for the one time that I went swimming there. I was out quite away in the harbor and was getting tired and had decided to return to the land. As soon as I turned to face the beach I knew something was wrong. The water had turned almost murky and was more translucent rather than transparent. As the first sting pierced my arm I soon knew why. Jellyfish!   A huge swarm or shoal had been pushed in from deeper water and now completely blocked my route to dry land.

I tried to make them out and could see by their size and shape that they were not Man of War or Box Jellyfish. The shoal looked about three feet wide and I believed that if I swam hard and fast I would get through them with little damage to myself. I was nearly right. I came out the other side covered in stings. It felt as if I had fallen into a huge patch of nettles. I look back and grimace when I remember the pain but know that it could have been a whole lot worse.

The holiday was soon coming to an end and thoughts of home started to surface in my sun drenched mind. It was now the end of February and our bags were packed. There was just one small problem. The Iraqi war had broken out. The news on the television showed Britain and America invading Iraq and we were warned that this may affect our flight home. It did, but thankfully only slightly.

After saying our tearful goodbyes we left Perth and its warmth and hospitality and I promised to return. It is not a promise I have kept, yet. Our flight to Singapore was without incident but that was soon to change. The first incident was one that I rather enjoyed even if it did terrify the passenger sitting next to me. We flew out of Singapore straight into a huge thunder storm. The plane lurched from side to side and a few people were sick. Turbulence does not bother me and it was well worth it for the view from above the clouds. Up above the storm we could watch the lightening as it headed downwards to the ground. It was something I have never seen before other than on television and it is deadly beauty without compare. I sat in my seat shouting "look! look!" as the lightening shot downwards from beneath us but the lady sitting next to me was not so impressed and asked me to be quiet. Noticing that she had gone a rather odd colour that not even her sun tan could hide, I agreed.

After about ten hours into the journey I looked out of the window and was surprised to see another plane in the not too far distance. It then occurred to me that it was not a passenger plane but rather a fighter type although I had no idea which type or for that matter which side it was on. I made the mistake of pointing it out to my mum who immediately went into a panic and called a stewardess. She reassured my mother that it was a 'friendly' plane and that it was just accompanying us for security reasons. In truth, this did little to reassure my mother who decided to calm her nerves by ordering both of us a large brandy!

It was not long after this that the pilot spoke to us over the tannoy. He explained that we could not land at our destination (I cannot remember where) and so had been diverted to Mombasa. He thought that there was just enough fuel to get us there!   I loved his positivity!   We did indeed land in Mombasa and as I looked out into the gloom I was rather shocked at what I saw. As soon as the plane touched and began to slow down several very young children appeared out of the darkness and with no thought for their own safety began to run alongside the plain. When the plane came to a standstill they were sent away by the cabin crew and I took the opportunity to catch some fresh air while the doors were open. The air may have been fresh but even in the middle of the night the humidity was unbearable. I returned to my seat feeling worse than when I had left. The rest of the journey was without incident and although we were delayed in the end by more than ten hours we eventually arrived safely into good old Blighty to the horrid sight of an English snowy winter.

Once home and acclimatised my purpose in life was to get a job which proved not as easy as I first thought. After a few weeks searching a friend managed to find me work at the company that she worked for that provided vehicle rental but needless to say I did not enjoy it. I lasted for less than a month. The company had its roots in America and had a completely different way of working than I was used to. I had to work with someone continually looking over my shoulder which made me feel that either they thought I couldn't do the job properly or they didn't trust me. The last straw so to speak came when I took a gentleman's details down over the phone but did not get a postcode because he did not have one. When I explained this to my line manager I was called a liar and incapable. Needless to say when the gentleman was called back he confirmed that what I had said was true but no apology was forthcoming. I felt that I just did not fit in and so handed in my notice.

My mother worked in the mornings as a cleaner at one of the pubs in the village and she managed to get me a trial shift there. On an incredibly busy Sunday lunch time I was thrown into the deep end and in just a couple of hours we took over a thousand pounds behind the bar. Before the fortnight was up I was working a seventy –two hour week with just Tuesday's off to recover.

I did have one holiday whilst I was working there. My brother and his wife owned a small semi-detached house in the Forest of Dean in Gloucestershire. They frequently rented it out to family and friends as a holiday let and on one occasion my friend and I spent a week's holiday there. It was an area of the country that I had never been to before and I fell in love with its natural beauty. For just under ten days we explored the surrounding countryside, got very lost in an area called Blakeney Straits, discovered many local country pubs and spent far too many evenings tasting too much local alcohol. I remember feeling quite sad when we left to go home but little did I realise how this small two bedroom house would end up playing such an important part in my future.

Shortly after I began work at the pub my cousin Gary from Australia came to stay with us and worked as Summer Assistant for my father and then also at the pub with me. Although we were pleased to have him his timing could not have been worse. Unbeknown to me there was trouble brewing and it was to have a profound effect on our very existence.

Although I enjoyed work immensely it is true to say that all was far from happy at home. The weir was at long last finished; something we were all very pleased about to say the least but with its completion came the news we were dreading. On the thirty-first of March we were told that the lock and islands would be open to the public from the following day. It was to be the one singular non April fool's joke that was to prove to be not only not funny but to be the cause of my father's slow and painful demise. In less than a fortnight the cracks began to show and my mother states on the tenth of the month that "Jim seems depressed as if he's had the stuffing knocked out of him." Relief Lock-Keepers who worked both with my dad and on his days off were complaining and stating that Jim seemed "Depressed." Towards the end of the month all Hell erupted when a large group of walkers found they were unable to leave the island. They said they had read the signs saying what time the weir gates would be locked but had chosen to ignore it. They expected us to walk up in the torrential rain and let them out. We refused but I was dully sent up after them and photographed them all (including an elderly woman) climbing around the gates.

For the rest of the summer incidents seemed to occur daily. The islands were just not set up for the public invasion. There were no toilet facilities and nowhere for them to get food and drink. In early May the National Rivers Authority as they were now called received a complaint about my mother. She had demanded in very, shall we say, blunt language that some people should get out of her garden and back onto their appropriate path. They did not like her tone and told the NRA so. The result was that my mother was ordered not to speak to anyone that had wrongly entered her house or garden, but to call one of the lock staff. She was furious but back-up from my father did not come. He did not seem to care about anything anymore.

I could go on and on regarding the incidents and I found reading my mother's diary for this year extremely difficult. My father sought solace not from his family as he should have done but from bottle upon bottle of whiskey. He drove my mother to a near state of suicide and on the many pages that she wrote I can tell she was crying either by the tear stains that have permanently marked the pages or by the shaky style of handwriting that show me she must have been trying to write while sobbing. However, even my mother who suffered night upon night of hideous rows and arguments can see that it was not my father who was to blame. I have often wondered how the Rambler's Association and the NRA justified their decision against the health, good standing and well-being of my parents.

In early June I saw first-hand the effect that this situation was causing my father when out in our local town Maidenhead, my father broke down in tears stating that he wished he was dead. So concerned was I that when we returned home I telephoned a senior member of the NRA and expressed my fears. As a result of this I believe that my parents were invited to attend a meeting with my father's most senior manager and promises were made to give more help to both my mother and father. I never saw any evidence of this.

The summer battle waged on with more problems being caused by the opening of the islands to the public. Access was only gained by the public on foot and so they would leave their cars at the entrance on the mainland. This meant daily phone calls to the police to have cars removed as we were now unable to go in or out to our own home by car. Members of the public would park in the small lane blocking all road access not only to us but to any emergency service that was needed.

The situation (which I have only learnt since reading my mother's diary) came to a head in the third week of August. I had to gain additional clarity from my mother. It seems that a particularly vindictive member of the public got into an altercation with my father. As my mother understands it a friend of my father came to his assistance. What exactly happened, my mother does not know but it resulted in my father being beaten up and him coming home in a state of extreme distress stating that "he had nearly killed the man." Who, we are not sure but the ramifications must have been felt for some time although my mother's memory seems somewhat vague.

There is very little to say on a happy note about the rest of this year. Working every hour at the pub gave me respite from the lock and all its problems and it is not until very late in the year that my parents find anything to look forward to. There is just one glimmer on the horizon for them and that is my father's retirement. With this prospect looming my parents start to search for a property that they can at last truly call home. In early December whilst house hunting in the Forest of Dean in Gloucestershire, just a few miles from where I had holidayed they are shown around a bungalow which as my mother puts it, is her dream. By the end of the year the wheels of property buying are firmly turning and it is not long before, for the first time in over thirty years, my parents once again own their own home.

My wonderful parents with my father poking his tongue out as always!

As for me, my future still remained unclear but it was not long before that was all about to change. For once Christmas was good. I spent it at the pub with the Landlord, Landlady and their family. With excellent company, food and wine it was a joyous if not slightly drunken occasion and one that will always conjure fond memories.

Chapter 16 1992 – November 1993

This year slipped in unobtrusively with hangovers rapidly being replaced by a non-alcohol related illness that left me in bed for several days feeling weak and not at all one with the world.

There had been no paranormal activity for the best part of a year and in truth I was not surprised. Although I was still living at home I was hardly ever there and when I was, I spent most of the time asleep. My parents were formalizing the purchase of their new home and as it was quiet on the river at this time of year my father spent a lot of time indoors. The 'activity' only seemed to occur either when I was on my own in the house or when alone upstairs. Both situations barely happened now. In fact there would be no more activity until the very last day when I left the lock, my home for the final time.

Working at the pub had taken over my life and the seventy hours plus a week were taking their toll. I am not entirely sure when it was but on a Sunday afternoon after nearly completing the best part of ninety hours I collapsed behind the bar and was taken home. I slept for the rest of the afternoon and for forty-eight hours after that apparently without waking or moving. When I eventually went back to work the landlady agreed to reduce my hours. My new weekly shift would now only last fifty-eight hours!

At the end of February my parents completed the purchase of their new home and this seemed to lift their moods for a while but it was not to be for long. With the onset of the river season my father spent more and more of his time on the lock and my mother was shocked one day to find a bottle of whiskey had lasted less than three hours.

The lustre had gone from my job and I now seemed to be continually unhappy and recovering from one bout of illness only to come down with something else a few days later. As a way to help cheer me up, my mother paid for me to go on holiday to Portugal with a friend for a week. We had a lovely time spending days lounging around the swimming pool and evenings at the local bar. We were staying in a villa fairly high up in the hills which was wonderful. The only disadvantage was that it was a very long walk down to the bars and consequently an even longer walk back up. However, it was worth it, just getting away from my job and the river was restful in itself. It was just a shame that we had to come home. Returning, I made the decision to leave the pub just as soon as I could find another job.

Early March saw the return of my cousin from Australia who started work again for my father on the lock. Although entirely coincidental, it was around this time that I left working in the pub and started work at our local cash and carry centre. The money was less but the hours were so much better and it was not long before I began to feel human for the first time. I could at last spend time with my friends who I had barely seen except over the bar on most evenings. It was a wonderful feeling going out with them and not being exhausted all of the time.

Looking back now at the events that unfolded from early on in this year which then came to a head in early July I do wonder just what the hell I was playing at. The answer was not to come until the following year but after the huge mistake that I made in going to Eastbourne a couple of years previously I really believe that I should have learnt my lesson but I didn't. A telephone conversation overheard by my mother confirmed her suspicions that I had been having a relationship with a married man. I had behaved appallingly and although as the old cliché states 'it takes two to tango' I was old enough to know better.

The full extent of our relationship came out over the following weeks and needless to say his wife was devastated. The problem was I was completely in love and I truly believed he felt the same. By the end of July we had rented a flat in the village which was just a stone's throw from where we both worked and I was sure that at long last my world was heading in the right direction.

Of course when anyone embarks on a union of this kind things are never straight forward and as my new man was also a father, his daughter took up a lot of our time with the worry of how our relationship was affecting her. She was about eight at the time and came to stay on many occasions and other than a few outbursts generally she seemed to be coping. Her mother however, had a different story to tell and so we always made sure that she was put first.

The summer continued as did our relationship and although all was well to the outside world deep down I felt that it was not going according to plan. Once again, desperate to prove that I could have a normal life I ignored the nagging voice of my subconscious and the odd disapproving comments from family and friends.

September brought with it the first tentative shreds of evidence that our relationship was becoming one sided as he informed me that he had to go back home for a short while, to keep his mother happy, so he told me. Pathetically I agreed, believing that by showing him that I trusted him would keep us strong. I was told it was for a two month trial, what his family knew or thought they knew was another matter as we still continued to see each other.

Back at the lock my father had put in for his 'run down.' This meant that he was one year off retirement and therefore just twelve months to go before he and my mum could start their new 'normal' life together. On one of my visits the Relief Lock Keeper approached me and asked me for my opinion of whether or not he should apply to become the new Lock Keeper at Cookham once my father had retired. He wanted to know what it was like living there, especially as he had two children of his own. I remember feeling a lurch in the pit of my stomach before I answered him and for some reason knew that I had to lie otherwise no-one would take this lock. I told him it was a wonderful place to live, the beauty of the islands was a unique experience for any child and one that would stay and enhance their lives forever. I failed to mention the spirits in the house, the trauma of the public on the lock-side and the fact that boat owners felt they owned you. I also missed out the fact that as a Relief Lock Keeper you left the lock to go home and that you only worked the hours that you were there unless you were on 'call out.' Once you were a Lock Keeper it was not so much as being tied to the job but the job being attached to you. It no longer became a job more a way of living and it was not a way of living that I ever wanted. He seemed pleased with my description and unhappily I thought that if I had just sold it to him then I could probably sell anything to anybody.

By mid-November things were back to normal at our flat. My partner was back living with me and on the surface all seemed well. I also received the news that my brother and his wife Shirley were expecting their first child which was due to be born in the following July. It seemed at long last our lives were back on a more even footing and normality seemed to thrive, for how long I did not know.

Winter rapidly approached and all was quiet and uneventful in my life. Christmas came and went with only little problems and I looked back on this year as a new beginning. I did not realize just how much of a new beginning it would be.

January slipped into February and with it came the realization that the relationship that I was in would not last for much longer but for some reason unbeknown to me then I took the decision to hold on to it like the proverbial limpet. A series of comments made by my partner's wife to me at the place where I worked (although extremely unkind but in her mind probably justified) left me very upset and confused. It seemed he was definitely lying to one of us although I was not sure who but with the clarity of hindsight it was more a case that he was lying to both of us and we were both too ignorant and in love with him to realize it.

The beginning of February saw him go back once again to his family, this time saying that it was for his daughter's sake. Although dreadfully upset, like the fool that I was I understood. I believed him when he said that he still loved me and as I continued to see him I came to stupidly think that it was better than nothing.

On a lighter note, one morning whilst in the village I stood speaking to an elderly gentleman who I knew vaguely as a customer where I worked. For reasons that I cannot remember he had to give away his pet birds and wondered if I knew anyone that would be interested. Unable to refuse an animal in need I offered to take them and so one afternoon a cage complete with four zebra finches (two males and two females) was dully delivered. They were beautiful birds and it was not long before I became much attached to them so much so that I thought their cage could hold a couple more. I looked into buying a

154

couple more of them but the cost was too great and so decided on a cheaper but all together better alternative. Purchasing a couple of nests from our local pet shop it was not long before the two females had taken up residence and a couple of eggs appeared. Without realizing it I had become a zebra finch breeder!

Sometimes in life it takes time to understand why we as humans put ourselves through so much pain and heartache even when deep down we know it to be a lost cause. It was mid-April when my reasons came crashing down on me. I had been taking contraception on a daily basis for several years and so the missed period of this month came as a huge shock to me. My periods which, I had been plagued with since the tender age of nine, had always been on time to the second so when this one did not arrive I had no hesitation in popping to our local chemists and buying a test.

I knew the answer before the two blue lines confirming the pregnancy even had time to form. Telling my best friend at the time proved no problem although her reaction was somewhat of a surprise. I had called her in the morning and had woken her up. Telling her my news she simply said "oh" or something similar and had asked to go back to sleep. Somewhat deflated it gave me time to digest the news myself. Was I happy about it?   What was I going to do about it?   In truth I did not have to even ask the questions as I already knew the answers. I was ecstatic and having a termination was not even a consideration. About half an hour later the phone rang and my confused friend asked me if she had dreamt the news? I promised her that she had not and she enthusiastically screamed her pleasure down the phone to me!

The next milestone was telling my family and of course the father of the child. I knew that he would not be happy but I if I am honest I did not care. He had spent virtually the past year of my life causing me nothing but grief and heartache and for some reason this I knew was why I had endured it. Still hoping that we may have a future together I told him that evening but even after all I had been through I was shocked at his response. I called him on the telephone and told him I needed to speak to him. He asked me what was wrong and I said that it would be better if he came round. In the end I had to tell him over the phone as he demanded to know what was wrong. To say that he was far from pleased was putting it mildly and his parting words before he slammed the phone down were that he would be around that evening.

It was a different man that turned up after dinner. He was so nice and kind and pleading. It was sickening to watch. He begged me to have an abortion and he was so nice to me that God forgive me but I nearly agreed. I told him I would think about it but only said it so that he would leave me in peace. The truth of the matter was that when he asked me to lose the child to save his marriage I knew I never wanted to see him again. He finally opened my eyes to the type of man he really was and from that point on as far as I was concerned his wife was welcome to him.

The next hurdle was telling my family and this worried me more than anything. My mother who was the first to be informed, once over the shock agreed to support me but the rest of the family took more persuading. My brother and his wife saw it as me deliberately stealing their thunder as there would only be six months difference in age between their child and mine but this, I promise was never the case. I believe it was just the initial shock with the birth of their child so imminent. My father however, did not take the news quite so well and refused to speak to me about it for several weeks. When he did, the conversation turned into a massive row and very nearly destroyed our relationship. It was my mother, once again acting as mediator who managed to get us speaking and make him realize that this child would be a blessing.

Although this would prove to be true my pregnancy was far from the wonderful experience that the relevant books stated it would be. Although I do not know, I believe that the term 'morning sickness' was coined by a man who had possibly never met anyone who had suffered from it. I was sick morning, noon and night and it lasted until after my baby was born. In fact I was so ill that at around five months I became terrified and went to see my doctor as when I was vomiting I was noticing that I was bringing up blood as well. The doctor explained that because of the violent sickness that I was suffering I had damaged the wall of my throat. He said it was nothing to worry about unless the amount of blood increased. At about the same time I also developed heart burn and with all this and a healthy baby growing inside me sleep became a rare commodity.

Meanwhile, I was growing rapidly bigger and now had no job. It was an odd situation. My boss had decided that the shop needed a total refit and was selling off all the food very cheaply. One morning I came in to find all the freezers being loaded onto a lorry and it was explained to me that they were being put into storage while the refit took place. I was told I would still be paid as he wanted me to keep an eye on the place and deal with any post that may come in. I readily agreed but for a reason that I couldn't quite fathom thought it all seemed very strange. The truth hit me the following day when I arrived at work to find it all locked up with no sign of builders but a police car waiting for me instead. It seemed my boss had had some financial difficulties and had done a moonlight flit. "Do you have any idea where he may have gone" I was asked?
"No," I replied but then the penny dropped. "Yes," I said quickly. "Now I know why I found yesterday so odd." I explained what had happened about seeing the lorry and finding it strange but not knowing why. "It has just come back to me. Africa is a long way to go for storage purposes."
"What do you mean," asked the policeman?
"The lorry, I knew there was something iffy about it. It had an African number plate!"

July arrived and with it came the birth of my niece. It was strange to see my brother now as a father as well but I had to agree that it suited him. I think they struggled a little at the beginning with sleepless nights and the adjustments that all new parents have to make but even if it does not feel it at the time any struggles that they may have had soon diminished and they settled down to enjoying parenthood.

It was now September and my father's last day at work was rapidly approaching. He was due to be sixty-five on the twentieth of this month and much of the house had been cleared out with just the few necessary items remaining. On the day before he was due to leave he was given a fabulous send off by friends, lock staff and boat owners on board one of the river's more prestigious passenger steamers. Even his cocky and light hearted comments could not hide the sadness he felt by leaving and both he and my mother cried at the fabulous presents they received.

The following day my parents left Cookham Lock for the last time and my mother's diary describes it as not so much as sad to be leaving but happier to be at their new home. With the car all packed up they left what had been their home for twenty-seven years to start their new life in Gloucestershire. It did not go quite to plan as they left without the two cats which escaped from their boxes and disappeared just before they were due to set off. I agreed to go and collect them and with the help of my friend drive them to their new home at the weekend.

That Saturday we arrived at the lock to find the two cats looking very bemused sitting on the doorstep of the house that was now locked up and to all intents and purposes, empty. The cat boxes had been placed in the shed and it was no effort this time to secure the cats inside and place them in the car. It was a strange feeling going back to the lock knowing that for the first time in my life it was no longer my home but with all that we had endured there I was not really sad to leave. We climbed into the car with the cats on the back seat and started to drive off. As it happens so often in the movies when people leave a place for the final time, I stole one last, long glance back at the place I had called home. Although the house was locked up and supposedly unoccupied I knew that for the time being it still was not. A black, solid shadowy form stood by the window in the upstairs bedroom above the kitchen. There were no features that I could discern as it was like looking at a heavy fog but it was definitely of human form. As we left the drive way I smiled up at the window and through silent tears mouthed the words "Goodbye." Perhaps I was a little sad after all.

Within a month work would begin on the lock house. Although it was a listed building it was deemed unfit for human habitation and so most, if not all of it had to be taken down brick by brick so that the interior could be modernised and brought up to date. I cannot remember how long this took but know that it was a substantial project. I did go back once it was all completed and visit. The new lock keeper Adam proudly showed me around his new home and I was dumbfounded by its transformation. The downstairs toilet and bathroom had gone and had been moved upstairs, central heating now warmed every room and the threatening atmosphere that at many times had almost overpowered me was no longer there. Whatever had shared the house with us for so many years seemed to have disappeared along with the wall paper? In truth it felt like a home should. To date there have been no reported incidents at the lock house that I am aware of and I wonder if it was due to all the building work? It is a theory that building work in a premises can often disturb and therefore 'wake up' spiritual activity and I think this theory has happened here, but in reverse. I believe it drove the spirits away.

However, the life at Cookham had taken its toll on my father. On his very last day of working he had woken up with a severe pain in his hand. This pain rapidly spread throughout his body becoming more agonizing by each passing day. It was diagnosed after several weeks as Rheumatoid Arthritis and within five years of leaving the lock it would take his life.

Chapter 17 December 1993 – May 1994

My twenty-forth Christmas was spent at a good friend's house where I woke on Christmas Day with very mixed feelings. This was the day that I was due to give birth and I was more than ready for it. The morning sickness had been dominating my life for the last nine months and to say that I had had enough of it was putting it mildly. Sleep was another factor which seemed to be almost a distant memory. However, after being told by almost everyone that I knew, that it would not improve for the foreseeable future, I had convinced myself that I had become my own personal expert in sleep deprivation and would be able to handle weeks without the blessed luxury.

Then, there was the other side of the argument which made the thought of giving birth almost unbearable. At the anti-natal clinic the mid wife that had the task of preparing all us expectant mothers had said something that had stayed with me to this date. She said "it was not called Labour for nothing. It was damned hard work." That didn't worry me. What terrified me was the health visitor's comment after my last examination. "It is going to be a big one," she commented after giving my enormous bump a good feel and prod. "How big," I had nervously enquired?
With that truly British sucking in air through the teeth as if I was the owner of a boiler that had gone very wrong and was going to cost me a lot more than the original quote she said "Ten, eleven pound, maybe even a stone." After that visit I had gone home and checked my scan pictures just to make sure that the child growing inside me was human and not a baby hippopotamus!

The family that I was staying with, I think were more nervous about the day than I was however, like many first time pregnancies the day proved to be fruitless as did the rest of the year. The last day of December gave me the realization that 'she' was to be a New Year child and it looked as if I would have to be induced after all. I had been informed that if I hadn't 'performed' by the end of the year I was to arrive on New Year's Day at the hospital at nine o'clock in the morning.

160

At around three that morning I had woken up feeling 'different.' It was an odd feeling and one that I did not attribute to my pregnancy. I felt very hot and very damp between my thighs but put this down to sweating due to the central heating being on. After all, when a women's waters break it erupts as a huge gush, doesn't it? Well, that is what I was told anyway. As we made our way to hospital the nerves began to set in at the thought of being induced as I had been informed that it could be quite a painful treatment. Luckily it did not come to that as my waters had indeed broken and although still in the early stages I was in labour.

After a long and at times agonizing period which lasted into the evening of the second day of the year I gave birth to my beautiful, perfect little daughter. I use the word 'little' deliberately as when she was born the midwife asked me how much I thought she weighed. I guessed at eleven pound and this answer was met with much hilarity. Coral Eleanor Fayth came into this world weighing a little over seven and a half pounds. So much for the baby hippo theory!

I stayed in hospital for only just over two days as I couldn't stand the screaming of other mum's babies any longer and spent the next six weeks at my parents' house in Gloucestershire. It seemed I had given birth to a child who had not listened to the advice on how to be a baby. From night three she slept for eight hours. She wanted food every four hours and was the most contented baby that I or, so they said any other person had met.

After my six week visit my father drove me home for me to live for the first time as a single mum with no help. I loved every minute of it. My life revolved around my daughter and to say that I was blissfully happy was an understatement.

At some point, I think it was during the February I went to stay with a friend in London and whilst there she told me about a woman who lived in the same block of flats as her. She was a medium and suggested that I went for a visit. It was dully arranged with the promise that this woman had been told nothing about me. It was a promise that I believe was true to this day as not only did she tell me about things that my friend could have divulged to her she also told

161

me things that would happen in the future. Those incidents have now come to pass with so much accuracy that it still today takes my breath away. It reinstated my belief in the spiritual world and I knew that even when I was on my own I was never alone.

Once back at home I continued with the daily chores that surround a young baby. I had to get rid of the birds that I had adopted but I had replaced them with some fish so other than looking after them and caring for my daughter, life was quite simple. There was just one problem. I had grown to hate the flat that I lived in. It was very old and in need of much renovation, something that the landlord and landlady seemed to have no intention of doing.

The main entrance to the flat was through the shabby kitchen with an equally shabby bathroom just off to the left of it. Out of the kitchen was the only bedroom which I had given over to the baby. Past the bedroom was a hallway which was really only an enclosed lean-to and this led to the lounge. The biggest problem came at night if I needed to go to the toilet. It was far from straight forward as it meant crossing slug valley!   Each night, after dark the kitchen floor and walls would turn into the venue for the international slug convention. There were thousands of them; all over the floor and up the walls, over the cooker, the washing machine and the fridge and then covering all the work surfaces. It was a Molluscophobiac's worst nightmare!

I had made several attempts at getting rid of them but each night like a scene from the film 'Zulu' they returned, wave upon wave of the slug-slimy enemy and I had no idea why. It was towards the end of February when I found an escape route from them but not in the way that I had expected. A telephone call from my brother was, once again, to send my life in a new direction and one that I will forever be thankful for.

The house that he owned in Lydney, not far from the village where my parents lived was due to have its rent renewed and the current occupiers were moving on. He asked if I would be interested in relocating to that part of the world and I said that I would think about it. The thought of moving to new, modern accommodation really

162

excited me but I was concerned at the thought of going to an area where I knew no-one except my parents. A further discussion with my friends reassured me that distance made no difference to friendship and so I gratefully took up my brother's offer.

The next month was busily spent getting ready for the big move. Boxes were packed and rooms were set back to their original condition. In early April once again with the help of my parents we said goodbye to Cookham for the last time and headed up the M4 motorway to Gloucestershire and the Forest of Dean.

We arrived just before lunchtime and spent the day unpacking and painting. I was determined that Coral would have a beautiful room before she moved in. By the end of the day all was where it should be except for the occupiers. We spent the first night at my parents so that the paint could dry and I could help mum repack up all of Coral's belongings. Although she was only just turned three months she was already fully weaned and she was beginning to show signs of speaking. Her advancement meant that she now needed more in the way of toys and just a two night stay at my parents meant she took belongings that would befit a six month old.

Our first day in our new home was wonderful. There were no sign of slugs and everywhere was clean and tidy. The kitchen although small, was neat and modern and it was at long last lovely to have my own bedroom.

Of course there were certain elements of my previous life that I could not leave behind even though I wanted to. The father of my child had decided to contest paternity, leaving me with no option but to take my daughter for DNA testing. It was a test that I knew was a waste of time and tax payers' money because unless she was the result of Immaculate Conception only he could be the father. Two timing, playing around or whatever other title you want to give it was something that I have never indulged in and the tears that I shed as the doctor withdrew a small quantity of her blood were not for him but a result of the anger that I now felt towards him.

I thought that was all I had brought with me from the past. With a new life in a modern house in a different part of the country I sincerely believed that I had put my experiences of the paranormal on the back burner. After all, a building that was only about ten years old and part of a large housing estate; with no draughts and no quirky oldie world design defects surely could not house ghosts or spirits. Or could it?

Within weeks of moving in, items began disappearing and reappearing in unusual places, sometimes days later. Then, when my daughter started waving at someone who I couldn't see and telling me about the 'nice lady' in the hallway and on the stairs I began to wonder. Could it really be? Was history really about to repeat itself and looking back now the phrase should have been, 'Here we go again!'

Epilogue

Over twenty-two years have now passed since I moved to the Forest of Dean and approximately ten years since I first put pen to paper and documented the first twenty-four years of my life. I joined the Dean Writers Circle in the May of 1994 and have been there ever since. This new path, although still being trodden has brought some heartbreaking endings and beautiful additions to my life. In the summer of 1999 my father passed away; the Rheumatoid Arthritis causing him a massive heart attack early one summer's morning. Although he met my then partner he never saw me marry and there is not a day that goes by when I do not think of my lovely, infuriating daddy.

I married in the Millennium and the following year gave birth to another beautiful daughter. My husband and I bought our first home just before we were married and moved again in 2002. Our first family home together was a mid-terraced property and then a couple of years later when our second daughter was more mobile we moved again, this time to a detached home on the edge of the town. Life, as they say is good but what of the ghosts?

It transpired that the home that Coral and I first moved to in Lydney was originally rented by a doctor, a female doctor who committed suicide. Make of that what you will. I can report that there was no activity recorded in our mid-terraced property. Where we live now however, has a different story to tell. On numerous occasions an apparition has been seen (both during the day and at night) by various people of a young girl wearing a long, cotton, nightdress. She has been seen and heard in almost every room of the house but as our children have grown older so her visits are less frequent.

My experiences as a child and teenager have stayed with me to this day and along with other experiences that have not been mentioned here have helped to shape who I am and what I believe. It is therefore possibly no surprise to learn that whenever time allows I can be found investigating alleged paranormal disturbances in a variety of locations. Under the name of ROPE (Researchers of Paranormal Events) I have even set up a small team of Paranormal

Investigators. I continue to be amazed at the experiences others and sometimes even myself witness.   The forty-six years of my life if nothing else has taught me one thing and that is there is more to life than death. Even more than us mere mortals will ever be allowed to understand.

I hope you have enjoyed reading
xxx

60792917R00092

Made in the USA
Charleston, SC
05 September 2016